'At a time when an understanding of wellbeing has arguably never been more important, Ruth's latest book is both honest and accessible, and helps us reflect on our own wellbeing and those things which can help to foster it.'
Jeannie Kendall, tutor in Pastoral Supervision at Spurgeon's College and author of Finding Our Voice *and* Held in Your Bottle

'Ruth's *A–Z of Wellbeing* is a treasury of thoughtful, practical and insightful perspectives on finding peace and wholeness. She is good at connecting with people, learning from experience, responding actively to the call to get involved, and taking notice of how things work (or don't) in practice. In this book, she has given us prayers, resources, poems, wisdom and much, much more. Ruth has grappled creatively with what it means to find wellbeing even (and especially) when life has been hard, and what she has learned is distilled and made accessible for all of us in the pages of this book.'
Revd Professor Christopher C.H. Cook

'Ruth has written the book we have all been waiting for – practical, wise and full of insight, it really is a wellbeing handbook for daily life. Perfect for all of us living in these busy and challenging times, I highly recommend it.'
Cathy Madavan, writer, speaker and author of Digging for Diamonds

'This is a deeply personal and highly illuminating take on the very topical issue of wellbeing. I recommend it very warmly indeed as both a tonic for the mind and balm for the soul.'

James Newcome, Bishop of Carlisle

'This is an excellent resource for all those concerned with emotional well-being – their own or that of others. By taking the device of an A–Z list, Ruth Rice gives herself scope to explore the breadth and depth of the subject. Her reflections are authentic and grounded, drawing on her own journey and on the significant growth of the Renew Wellbeing movement she has so passionately championed. The result is creative and compassionate – an inspiring guide. Essential reading for those engaged in the arena of emotional and mental wellbeing, whether from a faith perspective or not.'

Gerard Kelly, poet, author, speaker and
co-director of The Bless Network

A–Z of Wellbeing

Finding your personal toolkit for peace and wholeness

Ruth Rice

Authentic

28 27 26 25 24 23 22   7 6 5 4 3 2

First published 2022 by Authentic Media Limited,
PO Box 6326, Bletchley, Milton Keynes, MK1 9GG.
authenticmedia.co.uk

British Library Cataloguing in Publication Data
A catalogue record for this book is available from the British Library.
ISBN: 978-1-78893-237-0
978-1-78893-238-7 (e-book)

Cover design by Claire Marshall
Printed and bound by CPI Group (UK) Ltd, Croydon, CR0 4YY

Contents

Acknowledgements   vii

Introduction   1
A Lexicon of Wellbeing   11
Contents of the A–Z   12

Conclusion: What's in Your Basket?   297
Appendix 1: Mental and Emotional
    Wellbeing and the Church: Some
    Helpful Resources   303
Appendix 2: Rhythm of Prayer:
    Renew Centres   309
Bibliography   313
Notes   317

Acknowledgements

As I have written this book I have realized how much I am learning from my relationships with others in my quest to live the wellbeing way. Although the habits and practices I share here are towards having a *personal* toolkit for wellbeing, I could not have learned any of this on my own.

There are so many of you that have helped bring this book about that I daren't even try to list you all. Some of you I name in this book but there are many, many more. I want to thank each of you for enriching my wellbeing journey, for walking alongside me, for your encouragement and honesty.

To the amazing, growing, Renew Wellbeing family, I say thank you. Thank you for joining in the adventure. I hope you find this A–Z helpful as you continue to show up faithfully and attend to wellbeing where God has placed you.

To my own dear family I say . . . I am learning the most from you. I love you.

To my heavenly Father I say . . . this is all about you, all for you.

I thank my God always when I remember you in my prayers . . .
For I have derived much joy and comfort from your love . . .

(Phlm. 1:4,7)

Introduction

Why this A–Z . . .

This is not a book to define wellbeing. Others have written those books. It is not a book to debate wellbeing, they already exist. This book is my attempt to describe wellbeing. In effect it is a phrase book for a journey into a new land, into wellbeing itself. I have found it so hard to find a definition that works for me, but I have realized wellbeing is something I am discovering by living in it and seeing it lived out in hundreds of spaces. It looks like something and is hard to put in a sentence. So here are twenty-six ways of understanding wellbeing from what I see in God's character, my practices and community reality. I believe there is no greater need than a language of wellbeing at this time. I believe the church is absolutely key in the renewing of wellbeing in our communities, but that without a language that unites us with the amazing work of wellbeing God is already doing, we may miss this moment in history when the invitation to be bilingual, to speak the *shalom* of heaven into the need of earth, is clear and audible.

This is a book designed to be used by anyone who has set up Renew spaces to help them keep the DNA of wellbeing strong as they do the simple thing of being present, prayerful and working in partnership in their communities. A Renew Wellbeing space is a quiet, shared space where it is 'OK not to be OK'.[1] The first one began in September 2015 and at the time of writing we are working with around 200 churches setting up Renew spaces. We are praying for many, many more spaces to spring up. Hosted by churches, these spaces are simple, safe and sustainable and came out of my own broken story. You can read about all this in my first book *Slow Down, Show Up and Pray*.[2] This book does not require you to have a Renew space but it might encourage you to think about opening one or help you keep good wellbeing if you do have one.

But this book is also, I hope, an invitation to anyone with a pulse to attend to their own wellbeing, to write and live their own alphabet of peace. There is no greater task, I believe, than to find a language that enables us to speak honestly and live healthily together around the area of mental and emotional health.

This A–Z is my way of saying 'Let's all talk wellbeing, live wellbeing, be communities of wellbeing'.

I am using a lexicon approach because I love words. I know lots of them! 'Words create worlds'.[3] Words are more powerful than we think. Not just the ones that leave our mouths but the ones that rattle round inside our heads. I actually think the source of this quote goes back to the very beginning of time when God spoke and the world came into being. Whatever your personal beliefs about this, we all know how powerful words can be to build us up or knock us down. Words that we speak to ourselves can limit us or inspire us. These words that we think and speak become the bedrock for the formation of a view of the world and ourselves.

> This book is an invitation to anyone with a pulse to attend to their own wellbeing, to write and live their own alphabet of peace.

As a chronic, almost Olympic level, worrier, I know the truth of this. I know first-hand how the words in my head can dominate my day. Words about wellbeing are really powerful. So is this to be yet another self-help book about positive thinking for our wellbeing? I hope not! The intention in these pages is to open up some of the words I have found helpful in my journey of recovery from breakdown and in my adventure of learning to live better within my own skin. This is an ongoing language-learning sort of book. I am committed to learning the language of wellbeing.

I have not found language-learning to be an easy thing but a process that needs me to join in. I speak French but I didn't wake up one day and find myself able to speak it. I learned, I practised, I even looked at the book of boring verb conjugation. I lived in France for a while. I made hideous mistakes, like the time I announced to my new employers as a fresh-faced college student that I was pregnant rather than simply 'full' from the good meal they were serving me. They looked a bit worried about what they had got themselves into.

Since I haven't spoken French for some years, I am forgetting it. I had the joy of speaking earlier this year with a lady in France who is interested in setting up a Renew space. I had my bilingual friend on hand to translate, but amazed myself by being able to understand much of what was said. The problem came when I had to reply and I stumbled over words, had to find very long ways to say very short things and interestingly could not find a good way to translate 'OK not to be OK' which is at the heart of Renew Wellbeing's message. In short, I was rusty.

Wellbeing words escape us too if we constantly speak judgement, unforgiveness and criticism over ourselves. Languages need practising and learning for speaking to become natural to us. I believe it is the same with these wellbeing words I bring in this alphabet. This is a very simple way for me to try to share what I am learning about wellbeing. If we are to see it renewed in our communities, it would be good to know what to look for. So how did I learn, how am I learning, to speak wellbeing?

This A–Z is not a definitive definition of wellbeing but some language that has helped me; the importance of wellbeing for all, even when not being well. The definitions of wellbeing are many. Just search the internet and you will find 126,000,000 ideas of what the word 'wellbeing' means. For me, 'words that create worlds' need to look like something. Take the image of a seed that is planted. It takes root under the ground, but until it begins to surface we don't know what it is. For wellbeing to mean anything, I believe it has to look like something in my own life, our collective life and the world around us.

> I am beginning to believe that wellbeing is not something we feel or strive for, but something we enter into and that always exists.

I am beginning to believe that wellbeing is not something we feel or strive for, but something we enter into and that always exists whether we are OK or not OK.

One definition based on the work of the Office of National Statistics says that wellbeing is:

> Wellbeing, put simply is about how we are doing as individuals, communities and as a nation, and about how sustainable this is for the future.[4]

These are the best two definitions I have come up with for wellbeing.

One is a Hebrew word '*shalom*' which we translate as peace but on closer inspection is really much broader and fuller and deeper. It is wellbeing.

The other is the image of hands around a cup. The cup is our lives, our planet, our communities, and the hands are the bigger story of a God who is love, who is peace, who is wellbeing. The cup is held in wellbeing and then filled by that same wellbeing. Regardless of whether it is full or empty, it is still held.

But this book is not a theological, psychological or socio-logical explanation of wellbeing. I am not qualified to write that book and I will signpost you after each chapter to other resources that do this better than I could. I am only qualified to tell you my alphabet of wellbeing. I am only learning to become fluent in my own language of peace. All I hope to do in these pages is open up a way of communicating in words and actions that has helped me find *shalom* and has been the foundation of a movement of wellbeing spaces across the UK.

I do hope that this exploration of twenty-six ways to think about wellbeing will give depth and life to the Renew Wellbeing spaces across the country[5] as the church and community con-tinue to simply show up and attend to wellbeing together. I hope this will deepen the DNA of what already exists. But I also hope that many more, those who have never heard of Renew Wellbeing as a charity, those who have never consid-ered the gospel of wellbeing as relevant to them, might take the challenge to pen their own wellbeing alphabets, to become fluent in that which brings life.

In a way this book is a prequel to my first one. Unless we know how to speak wellbeing, to hear wellbeing, to practise wellbeing, our spaces and places with the name on the label will become yet another programme to run, yet more places for us to try to fix people. Whether this book results in more Renew Wellbeing spaces or not, I long that we would all make a priority of *shalom* as not just a concept but an active, dynamic, God-breathed language in which we are all fluent, regardless of the state of our minds and hearts.

I am hoping and praying that the journey through my words and what they look like in practice, both personally and in community, encourage you to think about or even write your own wellbeing words. There is no more uniting language, no more simple way to speak than the language of wellbeing. In a world that has faced a global pandemic, that has had the foundations of all that was safe and secure shaken to the core, we have all had to think more deeply about wellbeing in our own homes and lives. It is this journey that I invite you to articulate, and then maybe in the sharing of these words in our neighbourhoods we will be able to see and hear each other better.

I had a dream which I describe in my first book of me standing on a battlefield. That battlefield was the battle for the hearts and minds of ordinary folk like me. There was a deep darkness and its name was despair. The battlefield represented the mental and emotional state of many around us. In the dream I was plonked in the middle of the battlefield, ill-equipped but told to dance until spaces cleared around me and others joined the dance.

And as places cleared on the battlefield, I pointed to each clearing and a group . . . set out a picnic mat and sat down. A basket opened in front of them and it filled with good things from the skies. People around began to get up off the ground, put down their weapons, and to join in the picnic.

Clearing after clearing, picnic rug after picnic rug, we danced along the front line until, as I looked behind me, the darkness had become light and the battlefield was becoming a picnic site. It was glorious.[6]

This A–Z is a list of things I have packed in my picnic basket. These are the things, the habits, the revelations I bring to the table. These are the morsels of truth that I find sustain me in the middle of a battle for my mind. This is my little packed lunch.

Like the boy in the story in John 6 who was prepared to share the five loaves and two fish he had, even though it seemed ridiculous that they would be any use to a hungry crowd of 5,000, I am choosing to believe that these little offerings I bring might be blessed and broken and shared and fill someone's need for wellbeing somewhere. I am praying that they encourage anyone else squirrelling away a few scraps of advice and understanding to offer them up as well for the multiplication miracle. I am challenging us all, particularly those who call themselves Christians to prioritize the language of wellbeing, to share whatever they have, even if it seems too small a portion to be of use, and to see the picnic basket fill up with wellbeing ideas and habits, with enough to share with a whole community.

The layout

Each of the twenty-six letters of the alphabet will deal with a word that means a lot to me in my own wellbeing journey in terms of God's Word, my habits, what I have seen in community spaces, a story of what it looks like in practice (in these stories I have changed names, details and locations to protect people's privacy) and some resources that might help explore the letter further.

I have set this out with reference to the Five Ways to Wellbeing that all our Renew centres use to help us have a range of activities. These five ways that help with wellbeing came as a result of some research by the New Economics Foundation for the government's Foresight project.[7] Connecting, learning, getting active, taking notice and giving were the five things that people consistently said helped with their wellbeing. Using them as we look at each letter will help us to engage more fully with the word in question.

Connect: God has already laid the table for us, as it says in Psalm 23:5. So as we connect with the Word I will look at what is already in the basket, connecting to a bigger story of wellbeing . . . a gospel of wellbeing. These are timeless truths of what God has already given to us using Bible passages. Wellbeing is something that already exists and we connect to it.

Learn: What do I put in the basket? Here I will outline a habit or two that are helping me to learn more in this particular letter. This is a description of what I bring to the table of wellbeing.

Get Active: Here we explore what this aspect of wellbeing looks like in community. I will refer often to Renew spaces here but you don't have to have a Renew space to be able to practise these community ways of sharing wellbeing. What does community wellbeing look like?

Take Notice: In this section as we take notice and reflect together on the letter I will bring a story from my own life or from one of our Renew centres that is a good example of what I am trying to share.

Give: Here I will bring an offer of more help/resources and some questions to get you digging deeper as you give yourself to this letter. There will also be a prayer for you to pray in the form of a poem I have written especially for this book unless otherwise stated. In one case I offer a prayer written by a poet I deeply admire.

Who is this for?

This is for everyone . . . the language of wellbeing unites us. For some, you may not share my faith and I hope you still find some of the thoughts in this book helpful. You can feel free to skip the 'Connect' bit of every letter as we go through, if you choose, as this is where I will mostly explore what I call the 'gospel of wellbeing'. When I had a breakdown I was already a Christian, had all the resources of heaven at my disposal and yet still fell apart. It happens. I know that now. I am never going to suggest in the pages of this book or any other that coming to know Jesus, accepting the message of the cross and resurrection, entering into a new life in Christ – in short being a believer – will make all your mental and emotional health challenges disappear. We are still human. It took me a long year to even begin to realize this, to be vulnerable enough to admit I was not OK and to start to realize I had never understood the gospel. I had never really understood the character of God and I was trying far too hard to become what I thought others, what I thought God, wanted me to be. It took a hard year to help me begin to accept I am who God made me to be . . . on purpose.

This is a Christian approach but has stuff for all I hope. Learn a skill with me, get active with your community, take notice with these reflective stories and poems so that you learn to tell your own story. Give yourself to the journey of knowing what is in your picnic basket so that the battlefield of despair looks more like a picnic site of shared habits and hope.

When?

Start now! This could be used as a daily help, a 'one-off' deeper retreat idea, a Lent course (although you'll need to compensate for the shortfall!), a group exercise to deepen wellbeing language using questions as study guides, a year's worth of immersing yourself in wellbeing, learning a new language by looking at a couple of letters a month, or going through the whole alphabet every month and coming back to it.

How?

However you like. Please tell us what works.

On your own. There's plenty to try – lots of variety, as this is only *my* alphabet . . . write your own alphabet and share it.

In a group/as a community. With a reading group approach, this could be the basis of a new way of sharing life together.

It could start a Renew space or deepen an existing Renew space.

A Lexicon of Wellbeing

Contents of the A–Z

A	is for Acceptance	13
B	is for Breath	25
C	is for Compassion	35
D	is for Dwell	47
E	is for Empty	59
F	is for Family	69
G	is for Growth	79
H	is for Hope	89
I	is for Interests	101
J	is for Joy	111
K	is for Kindness	121
L	is for Lament	131
M	is for Meditation	141
N	is for Names	153
O	is for One	163
P	is for Present	175
Q	is for Quiet	187
R	is for Renew	199
S	is for Simple	211
T	is for Thanks	223
U	is for Unite	233
V	is for Values	245
W	is for Wait	255
X	Marks the Spot	265
Y	is for You	275
Z	zz . . .	287

A is for Acceptance

The LORD is my *shepherd* . . . (Psalm 23:1, my emphasis)

 **Connect**

Acceptance.

To be able to accept the day before me, myself and all that is in the cup of my life, others and the gifts and challenges they bring, I need to know I am accepted, loved and forgiven.

This is why I love the image of my life like a cup. Whatever the cup of the day holds, God holds me. If his hands are not safe, if in my head I have an image of an angry hard-to-please God, then I will have a hard job accepting the cup is safe. I will maybe try to be something other than who I am, be more positive than I feel, try to please more than I am able.

To be accepted is a wonderful thing, particularly when the One accepting you knows what you are thinking, everything you have done and how prone you are to wandering off.

In Psalm 23, a psalm I love and know by heart, there is a good shepherd who cares for, protects and looks after the sheep. All

> To be accepted
> is a wonderful
> thing,
> particularly
> when the One
> accepting you
> knows what you
> are thinking.

the sheep. He accepts them *all*. The shepherd doesn't decide which sheep need more protection, more shepherding than others. He shepherds them *all*. To know I am the sheep of this shepherd is the first step in my wellbeing journey. We all follow someone or something. I am so glad I follow someone who accepts me even though I have often displayed the same wisdom in life as a sheep.

If you have ever watched sheep, you will know what I mean. I once watched a whole flock follow each other through a ridiculously small gap in the hedge from perfectly good, safe pasture onto a road. Sheep do not always show the best judgement and do need shepherding. I know myself well enough to know that the acceptance and care of the shepherd is my wellbeing lifeline.

I love the parable Jesus tells in Luke 15 of the shepherd leaving the ninety-nine sheep to go looking for the one that got away. He would have been raising a few eyebrows among his audience, who would not really expect any shepherd to do any such thing: to value the one over the many. Who would be so reckless? God would. He values your life and mine so much he would shepherd us the same if we were his only sheep.

'The LORD is *my* shepherd; I shall not want' (my italics). Have a read of Psalm 23. This is total acceptance and care. Take a few moments to read it slowly as you start this journey with me.

This is acceptance.

This is safety.

This is the heart of wellbeing and the start of learning a new language for me.

Knowing I am accepted by my Maker then encourages me to begin to accept myself, and to accept the day as a gift, the cup of my life, whatever is in it. For this part of the acceptance adventure I need a daily habit – a more than 'once a day' habit.

Learn

Learning to accept the cup of your life

This is a simple practice that has worked for me. I bring you the word 'acceptance' and the phrase 'accept the cup of your life'.

The cup again! For those of you who are familiar with my work and teaching, you may well be asking, 'Is this all she has?' In many ways I would reply, 'Yes'. Although I will explore twenty-five other habits or ideas to try to aid wellbeing, this one is the simplest, the most profound and the most life-changing. You will hear echoes of this simple practice throughout the book even when I try not to keep mentioning it. That is because this is the simplest way I understand and practise wellbeing every day, many times a day.

This simple habit for those who haven't heard about it is something I started doing after reading Joyce Rupp's excellent book *The Cup of Our Life*.[1] It was at a time in my life when I was crawling back to some degree of mental and emotional stability after suffering a massive period of burnout.

To learn the language of self-acceptance I begin each day by making a cup of tea and sitting in the same chair, where I have my Bible and journal ready. I then choose to sit quietly and still and drink the whole drink while attempting to meditate on one short phrase from a psalm. I will talk in 'M is for Meditation' about this practice, but the act of sitting still and holding the cup once empty in two hands and just steadying my breathing (which I will talk about in 'B is for Breath') is an act of wellbeing. I sometimes even say it's an act of spiritual warfare. In the battle against worry and overthinking that is my constant state, I remember, as I sit still, that the world still spins on its axis and I did not make it spin. I can then say: 'There is a God and it isn't me.'

The hands around the cup are symbolic of being held in a bigger story; the cup itself has been formed and made on purpose, like my life. The contents are often a mix of more than one thing. The emptiness (which I will explore in a later chapter) a thing for me to accept, to embrace.

Sitting still or standing still whenever I hold a cup, which if I'm honest, I do far too many times a day, helps me to see what wellbeing looks like, feels like.

 Get Active

The language of wellbeing is universal, with many dialects. These habits and truths and helpful thoughts were not meant to be hoarded but shared, I believe.

> The language of wellbeing is universal, with many dialects.

So, we come to what this acceptance looks like in community. What can we do with this word? How will we share what we have learned with others without reverting to trying to fix them or impose our views on them, or even without wearing ourselves out?

For me this is where the idea of renew37 came from. You can read the full story of this in *Slow Down, Show Up and Pray.*[2] In an attempt to share what I had learned the hard way about accepting myself rather than constantly criticizing myself, I had invited others in the church and a few neighbours to meet in homes and meditate after having had a cuppa together. Just an hour a week, not sharing deeply what was going on in our heads just practising a new habit, learning a new language together. This was lovely and I commend it to you – commit to sharing this practice with a few friends so that you can keep holding each other to account and helping each other to stay on track. But for me it didn't go quite far enough. It still felt like an exclusive club for the few, and my heart had been well and truly broken, during my season of breakdown, for the many. I could not bear to think that anyone around me was in despair, lonely, or struggling to face mental health challenges without family.

This was where the Renew Wellbeing spaces idea was birthed. It was simply a desire to do what I was doing for my wellbeing that was helping me, but to do it in a place where others could join in. The Renew centre idea was to make sure all were welcome but that none felt they had to be the expert, or be put under pressure.

These spaces are delightful; everyone is accepted for who they are, not channelled into projects because of issues that we want fix. So often when I was in leadership I saw people as potential volunteers or participants for an idea I had of what community could be like. Even church leaders are prone to this controlling thinking. Dietrich Bonhoeffer in his excellent little book about community challenges this.[3] Renew centres are just a space to be a human.

Without setting up a Renew space it is, of course, perfectly possible to learn to accept others as we accept ourselves. I suppose I have found it easier to have a schoolroom, if you like, for this sort of acceptance language-learning. A place where it is truly 'OK not to be OK' and where we learn to panic less when people are indeed not OK. We can accept them for who they are and their story for what it is.

In our homes, workplaces and churches this is the aim, surely, to accept the other as Christ accepts them, as we ourselves have been accepted.

So what can this look like in practice?

 Take Notice

Walking past the window of the Renew space one more time, Sarah wished she felt brave enough to step through the doors. She had passed this way every day since it opened, this funny little place that looked like a café and was attached to a little teashop but on closer inspection operated more like a shared front room. She hesitated and placed her hand on the door, and as she did so, it opened and a smiling face greeted her.

'Hi. Do come in and have a look round if you like. You are most welcome. My name's Jo, what's yours? Sarah? Lovely. So, this is a sort of hobbies club for all. Feel free to join in. This is Michael, he's doing some furniture restoration. Bob here is playing dominoes, these folks are having a go at some watercolours, or you can just sit and watch. The kettle is on so do help yourself. There is a tea house next door that have some great cakes. If you wanted to buy one you are most welcome to bring it in here to eat. Just let them know you are coming here and they will give you a good takeaway deal. Oh, and this is run by the local church so even though we won't be pushing it, we find prayer helpful and there are several prayer sessions that you are welcome to join in with if you wanted to. The times are on the door and this is the quiet room where they will happen. Feel free to sit in the space whenever you like if you want a bit of "you" time. We all find it helps our wellbeing.

'Shall I make you a drink? This is Wendy. She's our champion knitter. Do you fancy having a go? There are spare needles and wool and we are knitting for penguins at the moment. I know. Penguins! These folks will tell you about it. I'll grab you that drink, then I'm going to have a go at sanding down that chair. So glad you could pop in. Any questions, do ask. Make yourself at home.'

During this gentle but clear explanation, Sarah found herself following Jo around the space and as she did, everyone smiled at her. Some said hi; others, lost in their hobbies, just nodded. She hadn't intended to stay this time, but maybe a cuppa and a few minutes with this lovely old lady who was knitting would be OK. She could always escape if they turned out to be a cult or something. What was the catch? How could this be free, without her needing to wait months for a referral? She had waited much longer in the system for much less.

The next week Sarah returned, stayed a bit longer, finally got the hang of knitting, and by the third week she found herself showing someone else how to do the basic stitches she had learned. It made her feel needed again, less of a project. She loved hearing her name spoken with affection, not disdain. In fact, if she was honest, it was a change to hear her name spoken at all. She had been so long stuck behind closed doors struggling to make friends, to cope with life. This was the first place in a long time where she felt at home.

Sarah eventually tried the prayer too and liked it. In fact, she liked it so much she found herself wanting to know the God she prayed to, and within the year of daring to stick her head through the door, she found herself believing what Jo believed, even though there had been no pressure to do so. She felt she was a host as well as a regular. She felt the slow blooming of wellbeing some days and had a place to belong even on the bad days.

She felt accepted.

Give

QUESTIONS

Which do you find hardest, accepting yourself or accepting others, and why?

What are your thoughts about God being your shepherd, about being accepted by him?

Where do you feel most accepted, and why?

Could you imagine a space, like the one described, in your community? Where would it be and what would you enjoy doing there?

PRAYER

Accepted
Loved
A place for me
Can it be true?
That one as great as you
Can know and see
My every thought
My fearful heart
Yet just accept
Me, all of me
Not start
to list the faults
To want me to be more?
Can it be possible
This bleating sheep
This fearful one
Has found an open door
A flock that makes some space
A welcome from a loving face?
Can it be you
Good shepherd of my soul
That you accept me
So I can accept myself
And be made whole?

Resources

Joyce Rupp, *The Cup of Our Life*. A six-week course in inner habits for quiet prayer. This is great to do on your own or in a group.

B is for Breath

 **Connect**

[God] breathed into his nostrils the breath of life . . . (Genesis 2:7)

Breath.

There is nothing more basic to life. We have learned that the hard way during a global pandemic. To breathe is to live. God has a lot to say about breath.

Breath is first spoken of in Genesis as God breathes over the waters and breathes life into the planet and then breathes life into the nostrils of the first humans. The Hebrew words *neshemah* and *ruach* are both translated as breath. *Neshemah* is used of human breath most often and I was fascinated to learn that at its root is the word for name or character, *shem*. We will talk more about names later in the book, but for now it fascinates me that our names are so important that the word for them is at the heart of the word for breath.

God's breathing gives life. In the New Testament, the Holy Spirit, who is God himself, is referred to as wind or breath.[1] So it is clear breath is vital for an understanding of how to connect with the bigger story of wellbeing.

With every breath we take, we are breathing in the very presence of God. It is why the practices around breathing that I will describe in this chapter are so very key to my journey of wellbeing. It's also why I struggle when people say they aren't good at praying. I feel like they are saying they aren't good at breathing. To breathe is to acknowledge breath has been given to us, to join ourselves to the breath that first breathed us into life and to share our breath with the air that keeps us alive. It is the most important practice of every human. And yet we do it without even thinking about it.

For me to pause and think about breathing, attend to breathing, slow my breathing and couple it with some words of truth to fill my heart – this is at the very heart of my wellbeing.

> To pause and think about breathing . . . and couple it with some words of truth to fill my heart – this is at the very heart of my wellbeing.

God's breath is all around me, His Spirit is in me. I have felt over these years of recovery like I needed to learn to breathe differently. He is all around me. I can choose to hold my breath and not breathe in his presence or relax, breathe in, breathe out and know he is the very air I breathe. His Spirit is not in hiding. He is all around us. This learning to breathe differently takes a lifetime.

 Learn

Learning to breathe deeply

So, what habit have I learned around this letter B, this breathing? I was born knowing how to breathe so I can't take any credit for breath as a habit! It may seem odd to have it here under 'learning'. But when I became unwell with burnout, one of the things I had to learn to do was to breathe differently. I had lots of voice loss and the occupational therapist assigned to me during my long stint off work (as a teacher) pointed out how shallow my breathing was. I had noticed this before, particularly when at the dentist. I have spent a lot of time in a dentist chair over the years, and it makes me panic. The deeper breathing techniques I learned during childbirth have stood me in good stead for my dental nightmares too.

But it is not just a case of breathing. When we breathe in, we take in the air around us. I think it matters what air we are breathing in. I can breathe in lies and panic and worry. Or I can breathe in words and thoughts that are good and true. This is where the Bible helps, for me. I believe it is the Word of God himself and when I breathe in and out, taking words that are good and true and timeless from God's Word, I find myself settling into the truth of these words. They begin to form me. They are more than words. It is like God breathing into me.

There is a verse in Isaiah 55:11 that says:

so is my word that goes out from my mouth:
It will not return to me empty,
but will accomplish what I desire
and achieve the purpose for which I sent it.[2]

This implies that the words themselves can transform us. Psalm 19:7 talks about the law or the words of God 'reviving the soul'. When I breathe in the Word of God, it does something inside me. The truth begins to set me free[3] from any toxic air I have been breathing.

Psalm 23 is one of my favourite psalms to use when a bit of deep breathing is needed. My dentist once asked me where

I go to when she starts work, where I zone out to. So I told her all about Psalm 23 and my deep breathing in and out of each phrase, taking the words deep into my being, slowing my breathing in and out, concentrating on just the breath and the words. I have tried doing the breathing without the words and I'm not great at it; I think my mind is so noisy, with so many words in there, that to use a phrase to breathe in and out to helps keep me calm. The breath itself is enough for some. Just becoming aware of the in breath, the out breath. Don't over-think it or, like someone I knew, you may find yourself having to blow into a paper bag through concentrating too much on breath!

I am no expert, except in my own journey of wellbeing. But there is much that has been written on this subject and I really believe we all need to learn how to breathe more deeply, particularly at times of stress.

 Get Active

As a community, breathing might not seem like a habit we can share. At the time of writing we are still keeping away from each other's breath; a deadly virus can make us scared of the air between us. I never would have believed I would be living through a time when mask-wearing was compulsory and we actively stepped aside when we saw someone else passing.

Breathing is obviously a collective act, or we would not have been so scared of the air between us during the COVID pandemic.

I became really aware of how powerful shared breathing practices were when I was in church-based leadership and trying to encourage the church to be more prayerful. I had invited every-one to come and pray each day at 9 a.m. in a borrowed space, a barn conversion owned by some friends. It was a silly time of day and not many came. So I called for evening prayer too. As I began to pray on my own, angry prayers of disappointment, I felt called to just breathe deeply and be with God. I eventually settled and was so engrossed in this practice that I didn't notice others arriving. When I eventually opened my eyes, the room had filled with praying people, all of whom had abandoned the normal chatter and words of prayer meetings and followed my example, just being and breathing. The air felt thick with the presence of the holy. I remember feeling I had to learn to breathe differently, to share the presence of God, to be open to my own practices affecting not just me.

> I had to learn to breathe differently, to share the presence of God.

This began our habit in our Renew spaces where we start each prayer time with a bit of quiet, some deep breaths, a med-itation. It can be the only time some folk sit in the quiet. Many are afraid of silence. I believe the local church is where we can be thankful for just the breath that we share. There is some-thing less scary about a shared habit with silence and breath prayer.

Many have said that our quiet rooms in our Renew spaces are so peaceful they feel OK just to sit and be; to just breathe. The very basic act of being human, breathing can bring us to-gether across the many divides of social class and different char-acters, to enjoy a moment when we begin to realize that God is all we need, his breath is our breath and all are welcome into that pool of life. It does feel like a pool.

I love wild swimming – well, any sort of swimming. There is a sense that a room filled with the quiet presence of God and each other can feel like a pool we dive into. And then we need to breathe differently. I have never tried deep-sea diving of any kind; I am told the temptation is to gasp for air but you need slow, long, steady breaths.

Shared breathing. Shared space. Shared air. We are not alone. He never leaves us. We share his presence with all around us. Pause. Breathe in. Breathe out.

 Take Notice

One of the times that made me aware of how vital this practice of slow, steady, breathing is really is a sad story.

At the very start of this embracing of new habits as I emerged from my breakdown, I met with a group of ladies to meditate on a psalm and practise the new rhythms of prayer.

My particular 'Cup' group – there were multiple small groups in people's homes doing this – was fantastic, as the host made a great feast of a breakfast and then we took hold of our cups of coffee and had a go at meditating on a psalm verse together. After the period of quiet we would not discuss what God had said or not said; that would be too much pressure. Instead, we shared how the time had felt, whether we had managed to stay in the moment, what had helped or not helped. And we gradually increased the amount of time from a minute or two to twenty minutes of quiet. (I know this would be too much for a Renew space. We advise thirty seconds maximum shared silence for a Renew group.)

This was a group of mostly Christians committed to the practice of God's presence. A lady joined the group with a friend. She was not a 'church' person but was deeply spiritual and talked about her deep breathing techniques as someone who had been a speech therapist. We had decided to honour each other, not to force our views on anyone and to learn from each other.

So we learned from this dear lady how to breathe more deeply as we took in God's Word. She in turn met with Jesus as we sat in the quiet. Sadly, she was going through intense cancer treatment and as well as praying for healing, we together learned how she faced her treatments using the breath prayer and psalm meditations we were practising together. We longed for a miracle but I was with her as she took some of her last breaths in the hospice with her family around her, and it was a miracle even in the sadness to see her practices come to full fruitfulness in those last moments.

Her decision to breathe each breath fully enabled her to take that last breath of shared air with us and, as I prayed and spoke the words of Psalm 23 over her, 'You shall not want', I saw her waiting to breathe the same air as Jesus. I saw her smile as she knew his breath was waiting to receive her breath.

I have been with a lot of people in their last days, and those who have practised breathing in God's love do seem to find it easier to let go of earthly air when the time comes.

This is a very difficult subject, I know. I have also seen people die in real pain and have not understood why his peace has not come. I am not trying to suggest we should all try harder to die well! But in this lady I saw someone who knew her very breath was her gift and she surrendered it back to God with such grace.

Weirdly, dealing with death has made me so grateful for every breath.

Give

QUESTIONS

What breathing exercises do you find helpful?

Describe a time when you were most aware of breath as an issue for your wellbeing.

What shared habits with breathing might help you?

PRAYER

Lord God who breathed life in us
The very air around us
The miracle of life
Is in this oxygen you make

And so we choose to still ourselves
To notice how we fill ourselves

With your presence every moment
You in every breath we take

From the first one to the last
In our future and our past
It's your breath when we are sleeping
You will greet us when we wake

Resources

Shaun Lambert, *A Book of Sparks* helps with Christian mindful practices, including breathing techniques.

C is for Compassion

Connect

[God] crowns [us] with love and compassion . . . (Psalm 103:4, NIV)

Connecting with God's story, I have chosen C for compassion as an important word in my wellbeing language. This is a word we use in our daily Renew prayers. Psalm 103:4 tells us that God 'crowns you with love and compassion',[1] and together or apart we choose each day to receive his compassion like a crown for that day. 'Love' is a word we understand but 'compassion' takes a bit of unpacking. The English word used here to translate the Hebrew word *racham* is from the Latin '*Com*', meaning with and '*pati*', meaning suffer. So the sense of compassion in the English is to suffer with or alongside. To have compassion is to feel for someone in such a way as to come alongside them and share their pain. This is what I believe God does for us. At the cross Jesus takes our suffering, he bears our pain. This is the ultimate in compassion. At the very heart of the gospel there is a suffering Saviour who knows and takes our pain.

Actually, the Hebrew hints less at 'suffering with' and more at this womb-like cherishing. This can be difficult language. The idea of a mother's love should be a birthright for every child but there is pain in this image for those without mothers, for those who have lost children, for those who have never known this deep, umbilical connectedness. I draw on my own motherhood to understand this word carefully and apologize to all who find this painful. But as a mother who has been well-mothered, I can feel the sense of this word deeply. When I first looked into the eyes of each of my three beauties, I fell in love in a whole new way; I had a deep inner connection. I would do anything to protect these little ones from harm. I had never felt anything like it. 'Fierce' would be the best word to describe the sort of mother love I felt and still feel. God feels like this for me, and for you; his compassion is that protective – even more protective; he is God, after all, and we experience just a shadow of what he feels for us. Compassion: deep and full.

The Bible is clear; the word chosen by the writers in the Hebrew language attribute to God a motherly, womb-like devotion to us. This would have been shocking language in a patriarchal society. But it's there in this word used of God:

> The LORD is gracious and compassionate, slow to anger and rich in love. (Ps. 145:8, NIV)

In the New Testament, the words 'compassion' and 'mercy' are used differently by translators of the Greek, but the sense of Jesus telling us to 'be compassionate' as our 'Father is compassionate' is right there – see for example Luke 6:36 in the New Living Translation. Mercy has more of a sense of something being paid for us. Compassion is more of a coming alongside and sharing a burden. But in essence they feel to me like the same thing in practice. He takes my burden, he comes alongside, he is merciful because he is compassionate.

This concept of a compassionate God who shares my day, holds my cup, accepts me and gives me breath is key to my wellbeing. As I sit and hold my cup each day, I can reflect on a God who holds me gently, with great care and love.

This compassion I receive enables me to begin to have compassion on myself and others. When I start to grasp God's deep cherishing of me, I find myself able to cherish others rather than just feel sorry for them.

> When I start to grasp God's deep cherishing of me, I find myself able to cherish others rather than just feel sorry for them.

 Learn

Learning to name your feelings (and accepting help to do this)

As a practice, compassion is easier to show to others than to yourself. I find it far easier to come alongside someone else's pain than to acknowledge and view my own struggles with compassion and love. I tend to view my own struggles as a fault I need to fix, or a problem that is mine to deal with. Self-compassion is, I think, a better way for me to understand my relationship to my own wellbeing than talk of self-worth. To be compassionate towards ourselves is still a novel idea to me. After years of self-criticism, it is taking some practice to try to view myself as I would another, or even as God might view me.

There are days when I don't feel worth much, when I know I am making bad choices, thinking stuff that is unhelpful and unkind. The beauty of the Christian path is that it is not yet another self-help journey. We can admit our faults and still have self-compassion. I find it such a relief to acknowledge negatives now I am learning to view myself with compassion.

One of the practices my dear friend and spiritual companion taught me is to weekly draw a circle in my journal, split it in four and write in each quadrant a feeling or emotion that I know is in me at that moment. My tendency before doing this once-a-week emotional health check was to ignore or deny any negative feelings and try to concentrate on the positives. But in so doing I judged myself for any negative emotion, and did not come alongside myself in my own struggles as I would another human. I am learning to acknowledge what is honestly going on in me and have a little bit of compassion for myself as I am, after all, human!

Self-compassion in both the English meaning which involves 'suffering with' and the Hebrew sense of deep womb-like connectedness have been very helpful images for me as I have learned to walk better in my own skin.

I can now spot when I begin to get mad with myself and pause and just take a look at what I feel, as if from a distance. I can't say I do this all the time, but I have found journaling helpful. I try to stop if I am getting angry or upset or generally feeling down, and draw a quick circle. The first thing I notice is that there are often other emotions in there too. We are rarely full of just one thing. Joy and sorrow can co-exist. This makes the negative feeling less overwhelming. Then I can name the feeling and ask myself what it's all about and just sit with it. Let it be what it is. I wouldn't try to fix other people needing to express negative feelings, so I am beginning to treat myself with the same kindness and at least talk about what's going on with God, my journal and, if brave enough, with a friend.

 **Get Active**

When I can receive his compassion, and be a bit more compassionate to myself, then I begin to be more compassionate towards others. I think before realizing I needed to receive compassion and practise self-compassion, my acts of compassion towards others carried a bit of desperation to be needed or to fix. Even praying with someone could lead to dependency on *me* if I approach that person with a need to help them, rather than compassion. In community we can learn a lot from how Jesus helped people.

In our Renew spaces, we start each day with prayer, asking him to crown us with compassion,[2] and then we take that compassion with us into the café space and the day. Even as I am writing this, I am aware that we can end up asking for his compassion just so we can be useful to him.

I tend to find myself grinning inanely when we pray these words 'Crown me with love and compassion' each day. The image of him, the King of kings, crowning me is so amazing, it is funny! What a wonderful truth. He is compassionate to me. He surrounds and crowns me with great love – even if I did nothing all day. He is compassionate to *me*. Wonderful!

I have found compassion flows better from me when I have sat with others receiving that crown for the day. It is almost as if we leave the prayer room as co-workers with God in his kingdom where the currency is compassion. That is all we hold in our hands, in our words. We have the gift from God of being able to stand alongside or sit alongside another human being and feel for them, with them.

This is a massive part of why I think Renew spaces work. They are simply places to see what compassion looks like in practice. They are not clinics to fix people. They are spaces where the language is love and compassion. Everyone begins to learn to offer fewer answers, to listen with more empathy and to just be there.

I think it can help that many people are not OK. We do understand where each other has been. The fact that there are no experts, no 'them and us', means that compassion is not a product we manufacture to give away, but a genuine response to finding ourselves together and broken.

I have seen regulars offer such wonderful support to each other without the hosts even joining the conversation. These spaces seem to grow compassion, maybe because we don't feel we have a lot else to offer and we have a lot to learn.

 Take Notice

I have learned so much from those who are chaplains or spiritual directors/companions. I want to tell you about a couple of friends who would fall into this category, and who have helped me so much on this journey. This is not to boast about how great it is to have these two Elizabeths in my life (they are actually both called Elizabeth, that is not a strange spiritual term for a chaplain, in case you were wondering).

The first is Lis my oldest and dearest friend . . . not old in years, you understand, but a friend who has travelled with me since the 1980s, with whom I have laughed and cried, holidayed and sat in silence through difficult times and great times.

This is a soul friendship of many years. Now Lis is a Baptist minister and spiritual director, but she is not *my* spiritual director. If you aren't sure what a spiritual director is, then check it out.[3] In a variety of forms, we have been seeking this sort of guiding and companionship for centuries. In the 1980s there began to be courses offered to train people to journey alongside others with contemplative practices. This was not a new thing, but it came to be a more recognized thing. I would highly recommend finding a spiritual director – particularly helpful for Christians, and for those leading others.

Lis does spiritual direction, but with me, we offer each other mutual support. At different points in life's journey it has been one leading and the other following, and then we swap, depending on circumstances. This is what Lis tells me soul friendship is. I have to say that I have felt so blessed to have met Lis in my early twenties, when I started a proper job and met the man I was to marry and since have had my kids, and a breakdown and a change of careers. Through all these things there was Lis. I walked beside her through valleys of cancer and the loss of dear friends and relatives. We have run into the sea together in wetsuits and spoken together at funeral services. I feel I have been the beneficiary of this friendship for all these years. I usually feel I take more than I give. I have learned more from watching this friend navigate raising a family and surviving cancer and dealing with loss than I have learned from any books or courses. I have seen her at her best and worst, and she has seen me at mine.

The word I use for Lis is 'compassionate'. She is a bringer of compassion, a model of compassion. She doesn't stand at a distance, even though she lives at a distance. She sits in the mess with me. An image chaplains use to describe what they do is to share one's cloak. She has often given me her cloak. I can't tell you how much it means to have this sort of friendship.

I am blessed with many good friends. I want to write about all of them, but I choose to tell you about Lis because I have just walked with her through one of the worst years I have seen anyone live through. She has limped through it with dignity, honesty, humour and grace and emerged at the other end scarred but determined to keep the faith. It is with compassion that she has let me journey with her so that when I go through the hard places she has already travelled, I will be able to remember that the end is in sight.

I know so many would love even one such friend. It would be so good if we all had a soul friend – and could be a soul friend – so that we may learn compassion up close.

So, I want to encourage this sort of depth of compassion, of giving and receiving through thick and thin. Compassion can look like giving something to someone at the side of the road in a one-off gesture, but it can also be the stuff of a lifetime's journey.

> It would be so good if we all had a soul friend . . . so that we may learn compassion up close.

The other Elizabeth walked into the church I was leading some years ago and offered to spiritually companion anyone in need of it. At that point I had never heard of this weird role and was very suspicious. But I took Elizabeth up on her offer. She was at that time walking with a Franciscan community and offered spiritual direction free of charge from her own lovely home and garden. The regular visit to her beautiful garden rooms were the highlight of my busy week. I would unwind slowly, sit quietly, walk the labyrinth[4] prayerfully, and use one of the thoughtfully prepared objects or booklets to enter more fully into God's presence. Then I would talk, just about me, for ages and she would listen and offer thoughts. It was wonderful. It was life-giving and it brought me through to deeper habits of the heart that formed the basis for what has now become a national movement.

The suspicion gave way to enormous gratitude as I saw the deep compassion, the coming alongside, the lack of judgement and the total acceptance that Elizabeth offered me, week in week out.

More recently she has taught us how to do group spiritual direction which we now use on our charity retreats so that we can listen to each other quietly, allowing silences, not offering advice but just sharing our cloaks (not real cloaks, just metaphorical ones!).

To decide to give this sort of compassion to another, just listening and offering and being present is something I have learned and am learning from people like Elizabeth, and the many amazing chaplains I have met in hospitals and schools and workplaces. To be alongside, to give compassion. I am so grateful.

Give

QUESTIONS

When has someone shown you compassion?

How do you show compassion to yourself?

How would you describe compassion?

PRAYER

Your compassion
Led to action
Your vision
Fuelled your mission
Those sheep without a shepherd
Moved your heart

The things that made you weep
Made change start

In all my getting active
Lord, remind me
You are the God of action and compassion
It's you who makes the change
Your work
No need for me to ration
My help
Enough for me
To join you
When I see
You
Your compassion
Lead to action in me

Resources

Check out the courses at Waverley Abbey College: https:// www.waverleyabbeycollege.ac.uk/

Or contact your denomination/church leaders for a list of spiritual directors.

$\boxed{\text{D}}$ is for Dwell

 **Connect**

Dwell in Me, and I will dwell in you. (John 15:4, AMPC)

D is for dwell. The word 'dwellbeing' is not one you will find in any dictionary, I don't think, but I have become very fond of it. I use it whenever I talk about wellbeing, as it holds within it one of the most important words in this alphabet of wellbeing . . . dwell. To dwell, to remain, to make yourself at home, to stay has become key to my wellbeing. As a timeless truth, something I have come to grasp from reading the Bible and getting to know God more, I feel this word 'dwell' is key for those wanting to connect with the bigger story.

In Hebrew the word 'dwell' is *yashab* which also means remain, stay or even sit down. I love the idea that the invitation from God to us is to dwell in him and for him to dwell in us. Double dwelling. In John 15:4 Jesus tells us that if we dwell in him, remain in him, he will dwell or 'remain' (NIV) in us. For many years, brought up in a Christian home, this was just background noise. It felt like an old-fashioned word, to be honest. But as I have come to love the word and the idea, I have dug a little deeper and now see the idea of God being our dwelling place and us dwelling in him as the most precious image I can think of. It is what the hands around the cup and then the cup filled with good coffee every morning makes me think of. Us held in him, him filling us. One of my friends compared us to being like the jam in the God sandwich. I like the image of safety that brings.

As I consider the word, there are three aspects that grab me.

Firstly, we dwell in him. I believe even those who don't know him are held in his love, made on purpose, part of a bigger story they cannot see.

In Acts 17, Paul is explaining the good news to some deep thinkers and uses their own beliefs in gods to reappropriate a phrase used about Zeus and apply it to Jesus:

'In him we live and move and have our being' (Acts 17:28). As he tries to point out that the God they have been looking for is made known to them in Jesus, he quotes this poem they would have known. I have found this so helpful. Our whole being is in him, even if we are not aware it's him we are looking for. He is all around us, holding the whole world in his love. How safe is that! But dwelling is more than a sense of God around us. His dwelling place is the whole of creation.

Secondly, we are invited to have him dwell in us. This process of being reborn, of inviting God's Spirit to fill and dwell in us in what some call 'conversion'. It can be sudden or gradual. For certain it is an ongoing process of continually inviting him to dwell in us. As a little girl I was taught the language of 'inviting Jesus into my heart'. I didn't understand it, but I believed it. I still don't understand, but I still believe. It's as good a description as any of what happens when we invite God himself, because of what Jesus has done on the cross, by his Spirit to dwell in our lives, our thoughts, our actions. So we don't just seek his presence out there in nature and others and the beauty around us, which we can do, but we also carry the treasure within us. We become his dwelling place. This is a 'profound mystery',[1] but one which has been so good for my wellbeing. In those dark moments of my breakdown, there were glimmers of this truth that began to dawn on me. When God whispered his love for me at a time when I was feeling useless and worthless, I began to realize he still chose me as his dwelling place so even when I couldn't see his goodness around me, when depression and anxiety overwhelmed me, he kept on choosing that dark place as his home.

> When I was feeling useless and worthless, I began to realize God still chose me as his dwelling place.

There is something wonderful about a homely space well-lived in, isn't there? Before I was unwell I never considered that my home, my life was a good enough dwelling for God himself. But he has spent these last years convincing me otherwise. I am the dwelling place of God. Wow! In the moments I grasp the wonder of this choice, wellbeing fills me. This truth in itself could well be enough for me, if I continually remembered it. I am his dwelling place.

Thirdly, he dwells in his people together. This is another mystery. Why couldn't he just confine himself to individuals? It would be much easier to make it personal and let others do whatever they do. But I don't think we can ever miss out the richness of dwelling that happens when we come together as a group who believe. God loves to dwell in houses made of people who are really different from each other.[2] The local church could still be his best plan for wellbeing.

The word in Hebrew also has the sense of 'sit down'. You know you feel at home somewhere when you take a seat even without being invited to. The Bible is full of references to God being seated in 'heavenly places' (Eph. 2:6)[3] and us sitting with him, and of Jesus sitting among people. A rabbi would sit to teach, so before delivering his wonderful manifesto in Matthew 5:1, Rabbi Jesus sat down. I love the image. A God who sits with us, among us, who takes a seat and then after he has died and risen again, he sits down again at the right hand of the Father (Eph. 1:20). In Luke 22:69, Jesus tells his horrified accusers that he will be seated soon at the Father's side. Then he says we too shall be seated with him in Ephesians 2:6. Imagine sitting down with Jesus! This is a great yet simple way to understand the concept of dwelling. Just sitting together; seated with God.

 Learn

Learning to sit and stay!

In terms of a practice, personally around this 'dwell' word I have one main one, and it is sitting down! I know that sounds a bit simple and I can hear you cry, 'We all sit down lots of the time, that's not a spiritual practice!' For me, constantly on the go before I became ill, but with a deep lazy streak that still exists, where I could spend large quantities of time sitting watching TV, this has become an amusing practice. My inner dialogue is constantly telling me to stop being lazy, to get up and do something, and often I can shut up the voices with Netflix and biscuits! Please hear me, it is important to be active for our wellbeing, it is not good to spend large amounts of time sitting down. I know that and am trying to remind myself of that. The coronavirus lockdown was particularly hard for many of us in that regard, wasn't it? But weirdly, the script can become a stick to beat myself with. It is almost telling me that unless I am doing something I am useless, that unless I am engaged in a task, or on the go, I am not worth anything; that only in doing am I validated. The act of sitting down, sitting still and just being not doing, is something I now build into my day as part of my wellbeing habits. Giving myself permission to sit down, to do nothing when I make a drink, to just be, means I can spot that the world still spins and I didn't make it happen.

When I was unwell, the very worst thing was the useless feeling of inactivity. So to choose moments of just sitting inactively as a reminder of that time is a wellbeing practice for me. I do it so that I never come to a point where I have dashed around so much trying to make myself feel useful that the only way out is burnout.

Sit down. Be still. Strangely, it's harder than you think.

Have you ever been to someone's home and they spend the whole time running round after you and don't sit down with you? I have been that person. So concerned that people feel at home that I don't make myself at home in my own house. This is what I am getting at when I talk about dwelling habits. It is the sense of making yourself at home in your own skin. People will feel much more at home around you if you are accepting of a bit of mess in your life and peaceful enough to settle with who you are in that moment. To be able to be alone with ourselves and the God who made us enables us to be hospitable to others, to make room for others.

 Get Active

So having said 'sit down and do nothing' as a learning point for dwelling, we now come to getting active in dwelling. This is a section about what dwelling for wellbeing looks like in community.

We put a huge emphasis on belonging and home in our Renew spaces. There are homes I visit where I feel right at home. In many of these places I could pop the kettle on, even let myself in. I could pull my feet up under me in a chair and be really comfortable. This is less to do with the furnishings and décor. I rarely see that stuff. I am not terribly observant and don't have a great eye for interior design. It is usually about the people I am with. I am made to feel at home by the way I am welcomed and the way the host sits with me, brings me into their world. This is what we are aiming for in our Renew space and why we call those who run them 'hosts', not workers or volunteers. We are hosting spaces that we also inhabit. We are dwellers too. In a Renew space, you can't tell who is a host and who is a regular; all learn to host the space together, as all learn to feel at home and serve each other. Unless we are at home in our spaces and enjoying them, it is unlikely others will feel at home with us. Sometimes we can overdo the serving and in so doing make people feel less at home. This is tricky for churches who have traditionally been the givers. Learning to make room to also be served helps all feel at home.

Getting active together to make a dwelling place is one way to respond, and there is help and training on our website if you want to join this movement.[4]

It is vital to try to engage with others in this dwelling habit. There is something very good for our own wellbeing to realize that we are never just an individual, we are always part of a community, a bigger group. Wellbeing is not just personal, and the idea of dwelling together – I don't mean living in communes, but dwelling in shared practice or sharing life in some way with others – is key to our wellbeing. One of the big issues I have with our mental health system at times is the term 'personalization'.

> We are never just an individual, we are always part of a community.

In essence this is a really good way to describe making sure each person gets the service they need for them. But in practice it fails sometimes to recognize that families and communities are a massive part of someone's wellbeing journey. In our centres we have sometimes been criticized by services for not moving people on into independence. It is vital that people can function when on their own, but I believe we are not made to be alone. God himself is three in one. We are made for relationship. So if folk need to be part of a Renew space every day it may not be dependency, it may be belonging.

To dwell together is hard work, too. People can be tricky. But unless we learn to dwell together we miss a vital aspect of wellbeing.

 Take Notice

I have spotted this dwelling in practice in so many places. Let me describe a moment when the penny dropped for me.

We were a few days into our first-ever Renew space project in Nottingham. I was on duty that day with one or two others from the church in the beautiful space the church had created. The bunting made of men's shirts was up (this was in an attempt to match the style of the tea house next door whilst being more welcoming of all tastes). The walls were painted a beautiful grey. The charity shop furniture had been lovingly upcycled. The brand-new jigsaw puzzles and second-hand games, the art materials and tools for woodwork were placed carefully at each table. The kettle was on and the mugs hung invitingly next to the sign telling folk to help themselves and leave a donation. The prayer room door was propped open and the meditation of the day left out next to the candle. The cushions were plumped on the sofas under the window and the leaflets and signposting table was full of inviting information for wellbeing activities and help locally.

It was beautiful and it had taken months of planning, hours of volunteer labour and thousands of pounds from generous church people's pockets. And now it was ready. I stalked around touching everything, writing up the times for prayer on the chalkboard, making a cuppa. We had done morning prayer and it was lovely, but an hour in I was really unsettled. What if no one came? What if this was just a huge waste of time? Why was I here when I could be getting on with something at home?

Across the anxiety I heard Hannah's voice. 'Ruth, come and sit down and do this origami with us.' Not being a fan of origami and wanting to be ready if someone came to the door, I shook my head and continued to stalk. Eventually Hannah's insistence won through. What a gift she was to me. I eventually sat down at the table with the two other people there that day, both Christians, still asking myself what we thought we were doing when there was a world out there needing saving. How would origami help!

My inner dialogue took a bit of shutting up, but after an hour I had begun to settle, to learn a new skill, to listen more to the stories others told and the sound of my own breathing, to dwell. I was the project in those early days. Hannah, who was really unwell with her mental health at the time, was my teacher. I had to learn to dwell, to sit down, to be present at least to myself if I was ever to be present to anyone else. I had to learn by being, not just doing. By becoming. It is an ongoing project. But the fruit of learning to be at home in myself and with others has been wonderful.

Give

QUESTIONS

What does the word 'dwell' mean to you? What pictures or images does it bring up for you?

Where and when do you feel most at home, and why?

What habits do you have for dwelling? Do you sit still often, or does it look different for you?

How do you feel about being God's dwelling place?

What space do you dwell in with others, or what habits join you to others?

PRAYER

Dwell in me
As I dwell in you
Great host of this table
In pastures new
Help me accept that you want in
You choose my home, my life
Despite my sin
And as I'm racing up and down
To try to smile and erase that frown
You whisper
I have come to dwell in you
Just as you are, so
Child, please come, sit down too

Resources

Greg Boyd, *Present Perfect*. This is a book full of ideas and habits to help us dwell in each present moment more. Pick one and try it.

E is for Empty

 **Connect**

[Jesus] emptied himself . . . (Philippians 2:7, NRSV)

As a wellbeing word, this word 'empty' may seem a bit negative to you. However, I have come to accept that emptiness and self-emptying is at the heart of wellbeing for me.

Have you ever got to that point when you are dehydrated but haven't noticed it? I have. Times when I forget to drink water and then get a headache and feel weary but still don't realize and take a drink. People have had to be hospitalized for dehydration. It's a serious business. Water is life.

Thirst, emptiness of water, is only good if it makes us drink. I have also been empty and filled myself on things that don't satisfy hunger or thirst properly. Have you?

This concept of emptiness as something to embrace was new to me. I had a season of enforced emptiness and could only think of passages in the Bible about fullness. My sense of being broken and empty therefore made me feel more of a failure. I would panic and try to fill up on activity, helping others, busyness. But the thirst deep down was for something more satisfying, eternal.

So I have become quite fascinated by a little phrase in Philippians 2 that talks about Jesus 'emptying' himself. The Greek word here is *kenosis*, self-emptying. This is a word that, when used elsewhere in the Bible, has negative connotations and can be translated as doing something 'in vain', something being pointless or void. So to see it used here to speak of what Jesus did in coming to earth and becoming human and dying on a cross is sobering. Those of us who follow Jesus know we follow the way of the cross, but our talk is often around the life and joy he brings, the purpose and love. This is all true but I had forgotten, or never understood, that the way of the cross, the way of Jesus, is a way of being emptied of everything. Jesus gives up heaven, he gives in to human limitations, he gives up his life. So as we follow him it will not be surprising when there is loss, emptying of self and sin and ultimate control.

Think of what it meant for him to empty himself for us. The only way for him to rescue humanity was to become one of us, die our death for us. He could see we were not OK, would never be OK without him, and so he gave up the big OK of heaven itself to bring it to us so that we could be held in his bigger story which is always OK – more than OK. This is why it is OK for me every day to not be OK. He has emptied himself so that when I am empty, he can fill me.

It is why when I have felt most empty, most lost, I have often encountered God's presence in the most profound ways. It is why when I have met people who have lost everything but still somehow trust Jesus, they seem to me to be the richest people of all. This is a topsy-turvy kingdom with a King who empties himself. This is good news for the empty and the broken and the lost, and a challenge to take up a daily habit of self-emptying for the overfull and over-busy ones.

> When I have felt most empty, most lost, I have often encountered God's presence in the most profound ways.

Learn

Palms down, palms up

One habit for this word 'empty' that I practise daily is again with my cup. It does seem that such a lot of my wellbeing is drawn into one basic image. I think I have such a cluttered mind that it helps to have a really simple practice. It may be simple, but it has depth and many facets. I take my cup, I drink my drink and then I sit still and hold the now empty cup in both hands. The symbolism is of the cup as my life and the hands as God's. But the emptiness, looking into the now empty cup and accepting the emptiness, is also part of my meditation practice. If I have a busy day I take a bigger cup so I have to sit longer to drink, and then see more emptiness and more need for filling.

This habit of accepting emptiness reminds me of darker days, times when I have felt I had nothing, could do nothing. Instead of running from those memories, I accept them and remember I got through that. The emptiness filled up and it was only through emptiness that I made space for real peace, real *shalom*, real wellbeing. This simple habit means that I try not to panic when I feel I have nothing, when I can't handle something. I try just to recognize and name it. Then I ask God to fill me with his love and compassion. This is a morning practice but can be repeated at any time of the day. If you can attach an inner practice to an outer activity or object that you see or use frequently, you will be reminded often to acknowledge your own need and allow God to fill you.

The other practice I have is 'palms down, palms up'. I can have cluttered thoughts, worried inner mess. So I sit with hands facing up and imagine all these people and thoughts in my hands and then when ready, turn my hands over and imagine the things I carry being placed into God's bigger hands. I don't just drop them; they are important. I hand them over. Then I turn my empty hands back over and receive peace. This can take a few turns, even with one thought or person I'm worrying about. You don't have to do the hands thing, you can just picture it, but I think involving your body can help engage your mind. It helps me, anyway. You might have your own habits. The important thing for me is not to be afraid of emptiness.

A word here about this practice. I don't ever empty my mind in meditation as some practices would have you do. Personally I feel safer replacing what is cluttering my mind with a true and good thought or phrase.

 **Get Active**

Together in community this practice of emptying is at the heart of being able to receive the gift of the other. Before setting up renew37, a quiet shared space for all to come and attend to their wellbeing,[1] I think I believed that my job as a Christian was to always have something to give others, always have an answer. I am learning that this can shut down other people's opportunities to give, which is essential to our wellbeing. So to leave some room even in the planning of a Renew space for the ideas of others, to ask for help, to come empty is not always a bad thing. It can offer others the chance to give, to fill your cup. Be honest when you don't have an answer and see what help emerges in the room. It can be from really unlikely sources.

Two phrases we use in Renew Wellbeing come from this emptying and filling image.

Co-production is a word used a lot in statutory services, meaning to create a service together; not to be done unto, but to work with. I am really keen on this idea. I believe God chooses this way of operating with us. But for co-production to work it requires those who think they know what things should look like, those who are in power or in charge, to empty out a bit of space, to leave room for what others bring.

In our Renew spaces we try to encourage all to bring and share a hobby as a simple way to honour what each person holds and stands for. This is one way in which emptying some space brings wellbeing. It can be a bit scary to have less organization, fewer planned activities, but in leaving room the variety and creativity increases.

The other term we use a lot is *people of peace*. Jesus used this expression, maybe in different words, when he instructed the disciples to go out and preach the gospel of the kingdom. He told them to take nothing with them, to find people who would welcome them, to receive the hospitality offered and to speak peace on these people (Matt. 10:7–13). This willingness to go empty, to receive help, to find people who have something to give and accept what they offer – this is quite a long way from what churches do. For all the right reasons we often go with lots of answers and offers and look for the emptiness in others. Jesus here turns that on its head and says we need to be willing to go empty, to be willing to receive as well as give.

> We need to be willing to go empty, to be willing to receive as well as give.

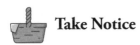 **Take Notice**

The best example of this in my own life is an occasion I have written about before. This is an intensely vulnerable thing to share but that is what emptiness is, vulnerability in practice.

It was a moment half way through the year I spent struggling with low mood, anxiety and burnout. I often stayed in bed, hiding from the world, unable to cope with the simplest of tasks. This day was no exception. I lay there listening to my children being cared for very capably by my wonderful husband. I cried with shame that I couldn't seem to join in the day with them. I switched on the TV to drown out my critical thoughts. This pattern of behaviour had lasted for so many weeks, I had lost count. I knew people were worried about me. *I* was worried about me. The voice loss I had been experiencing for many months gave me somewhere to hide, a reason to stay in bed. I cried out to God for my voice back at times, but I had my fingers crossed in case he answered. I couldn't go back to what my life was. It was too much for me. I could not imagine doing anything else except staying here in my room. If I rested enough I would be able to cope with some time with the children after school.

I lay there watching yet another rerun of an American soap. I wasn't thinking any deep, meaningful thoughts, I wasn't even crying out that day for God's presence. I was completely empty, completely lost.

And that is when it happened. At my lowest point. I suddenly became aware of what I can only describe as the arms of God holding me, wrapped around me. As the presence increased in the room, the sound of the TV became irrelevant and I heard an audible whisper in my ear. I believe to this day it was the voice of God. Right there with me, in a not very spiritual moment, an empty moment, my lowest moment, saying, 'Ruth, I couldn't love you any more than I do right now and I will never love you any less.'

This was the moment I describe as being born again all over again. The sudden realization that 'This is what the gospel is. This is what God's love is like. I can't earn it; I don't deserve it. He is not saying "try harder", or "you can do this"'. This was no great motivational speech. It was pure, undeserved love at a time when I was doing nothing for him.

This is wellbeing. I am loved. Full stop.

Anything else I managed to do or be from that point on would be a bonus. I had heard in that whisper that if I never managed to get up again, God was not disappointed in me. He loved me. Utterly and completely. In that moment that was enough. In every moment since I remind myself that it is still enough.

It was many months before I eventually felt well enough to return to work and life, and even then, big changes were needed. I could not manage the life I had lived. But that empty moment defined how I now understand the need to keep coming back to him empty. That moment redefined all I believe about myself and about God.

Give

QUESTIONS

What experiences have you had of feeling empty?

What do you turn to, to fill yourself up?

How does it make you feel to go empty-handed into a situation?

PRAYER

Fear or no fear
I choose to believe
Trembling and hiding
And reaching through the crowd[2]
Not daring draw attention
To my shame

Or publicly announcing
You're the only one I need
And pleading for your help
I come again
Daring to believe
I reach out
To touch the space
Where I'm sure you must be waiting
Just for me

I bring my empty heart
Throwing caution at your feet
There are moments when I simply have to be
Here
Fully present
Fully broken
Fully empty!
Believing in the message of the cross
Where not seeing is believing
But believing leads to seeing
I bring you all my weariness and loss

And fear or no fear
Faith or no faith
You reach out
And fill my empty space
With Holy Spirit breath
And joy that conquers death
And choosing to believe
I glimpse your face

Resources

There are some great resources to access around rhythms and habits of life from various retreat centres including:

Celtic Daily Office, Northumbria Community: https://www.northumbriacommunity.org/offices/how-to-use-daily-office/

F is for Family

Connect

[You set] the lonely in families . . . (Psalm 68:6, NIV)

F is for family. This will make some people instantly uncomfortable and I am sorry for that. The idea of family is great for some and very painful for others. But one of our big hopes in our Renew movement is that people will find a place to belong where they are known and loved by name not label. This is family for me.

> One of our big hopes in our Renew movement is that people will find a place to belong where they are known and loved by name not label.

This wellbeing journey is hard to do in a vacuum. I think God believes in family too. Trinity is three in one; God is in himself a family. One of the verses that has been key for us at Renew Wellbeing is Psalm 68:6 where the psalmist says that God 'sets the lonely in families' (NIV) and sets the captives free.

My understanding of God's heart for our wellbeing has family written all over it.

Firstly, he is relational. He is Father, Spirit and Son. The Trinity teaching invites us to become one with a God who is present in three persons. I remember as a child and young person finding this all very confusing and having great debates about who we should be praying to. The older I get, the more I love the truth of the Trinity. I love that we are made in the image of a God who is at his very heart in relationship with himself. It's a mystery, sure enough, but a beautiful one that makes me even more glad I follow such a God that is not just a distant deity but a Father, a friend in human skin and a Spirit who can live in me. I love that from the very beginning of time we see all three persons of the Trinity working together. At Jesus' baptism, the Holy Spirit descends and the voice of the Father is heard. All three persons are present at one time.[1]

I love the story in Genesis 18 where the three strangers meet with Moses. The description of this encounter under a tree introduces us to a God who is three persons. This is beautifully depicted in Rublev's icon[2] which shows the Trinity sitting at a table with a space left for you, for me. I often say to my Renew centre hosts in training, 'You are not the host at the Renew centre; you are invited to sit and join in by the real host: Father, Spirit, Son.'

Secondly, he made us to be in relationship. He says when he makes man, 'It is not good for the man to be alone.'[3] This sentence stands out in contrast to all the declarations of how good everything is that God is saying as he creates. This is the only time he says it isn't good and it is about isolation. All the way through the Old Testament there are instructions for households and family relationships and tribes and people groups. In the New Testament the same teachings exist, plus a whole new language around becoming family, 'one anothering', loving each other, and widening the family circle to include those who are alone. Jesus invites people to leave their families and follow him, of course, but he is also part of a family. His mother is there at the cross and one of the few sentences he speaks as he dies is to make sure she is looked after in a new family, asking John to be a son to her (John 19:26,27). This encounter, this care for his earthly mother, this instigation of a new family order is a beautiful thing.

Thirdly, we are called God's children and he is our Father. In 1 John 3:1 it says, 'See what kind of love the Father has given to us, that we should be called children of God; and so we are.' The language is very clear. This is family language and we are the family. If God is Father, then we are all related to each other and there is room in that family for all. The glorious parable of the prodigal son in Luke 15 draws us deeply into a narrative of family, a dysfunctional family at that. Here is deep love and forgiveness and acceptance coupled with jealousy and rivalry set in a family context to help us understand our relationship with God.

Family as an important aspect of wellbeing is key. It's why we have church. Church is not a place, but the people of God being the community of *shalom* in the way they are family, showing what sort of Father they have. It is why I feel the local church needs to be at the heart of any wellbeing movement. And it is why the church needs to learn to be family even more and open up its heart and its practices to all in these days when wellbeing is in short supply.

 Learn

You can't choose your family . . . or maybe you can?

It is so important to live this wellbeing stuff out together. Maybe your family isn't the best place to start; families can be tricky. I am so grateful for mine but recognize this is a difficult area for many. But I know I need not just my family but also a church family. Here I learn about how to love those different to me. The church is the family we choose, even when it feels hard to belong. Vulnerability is learned if we stick with a group of people (unless, of course, it is toxic for you . . . then choose again). I happen to believe the local church family could still be the best hope for the nations, could be the most beautiful expression of community, could be the best visible practice of wellbeing. The church is indeed the body of Christ here on earth.

So, what habits can we learn together? What habit/practice denotes family for me? I am not saying I have come from a perfect family or have raised one. Far from it. My family would agree! We have loved and fought, had great days and bad ones. I have been a terrible mother and a good one. We are the project. I am the project. But I am so glad to have had such wonderful people to learn family with.

I am pretty sure the perfect Christian family does not exist. I chased after that unreality for far too many years and it made me shouty and anxious. I am learning that wellbeing in family is a lifelong project, a language we learn by babbling rubbish, making mistakes and saying sorry a lot. Someone asked me the other day what advice I would give to young parents about contemplative practices and living peacefully. I laughed and suggested they were asking the wrong person. There have been seasons in my life where I have found it impossible to slow down, show up and pray, as my last book suggests we should all do. Those seasons have passed and I look back and see the rich seam of learning that was there. But at the time . . . we all just did our best and God showed up despite that.

I have a lovely family and still fell apart. Many of you have so much less, have difficult family relationships, loss and heartache and you are managing fine. I know, it makes no sense to me either! But it makes me sad to hear stories of toxic families and terrible loss.

The idea of family being beyond blood is so key to me. The family of God is vast; there is room for all. Every local church, every community of believers, every Renew space has a place set at the table for the stranger.

I need to be part of a community even when I don't want to or can't be bothered. It can be an effort to make myself vulnerable to others, and easier to go it alone. But a choice to belong includes many little decisions to attend a session, pick up a phone, confront a misunderstanding, forgive an offence.

 ## Get Active

This reality of family is the most important activity of the church, alongside prayer, I believe. By that I don't just mean helping families of origin, but becoming a family of choice that embraces all.

> Family is the most important activity of the church, alongside prayer.

In my life, that has looked like making sure I stay in touch with my blood family, learning to love them without controlling them. But it has also looked like always being part of a church family, even when it was hard to do so. The church is no more a perfect family than a nuclear family is. A lot of criticism is levelled at the church, as if it is a business or a club. But it is a family and is made up

73

of ordinary people with faults. The point of the family unit is to provide a safe place for us to grow and learn. The church should be no different. In many ways I am sad that Renew spaces have been necessary at all. Every church should be the safest place and group of people for anyone who is struggling with their mental and emotional health. Our grasp of our own sin should make us the best family to belong to, without judgement and with great love. However, our families of faith are just as dysfunctional at times as our blood families.

In our Renew spaces we have attempted to make the belonging as easy as possible by making each space work well for the most anxious, most isolated person. I often describe what a Renew space looks like by describing Christmas day in our house. One person is doing a jigsaw, a couple of others are playing a game, someone is asleep in a chair but we all belong and there is room for all. I truly believe these shared spaces would help any church to be present consistently and without damage to their own wellbeing. It is a way of being family while still looking after your personal wellbeing. There are times when being together as a family can be too much or at times, even dangerous. The shared values of our Renew spaces allow folk to join a family-type group safely and sustainably.

This is, of course, also possible in our own families and homes. Many people have moved over to make space for another in their family unit. It's a beautiful thing. But when someone is feeling unwell, particularly with their mental health, it can help to have more boundaries in the approach to shared life.

The trouble with our existing ways to join in with the family that is church, or even our own families, is that it can feel 'all or nothing'. When someone feels overwhelmed by people and life, it can be tempting to just draw back from everyone – even from the family that wants to include them. They need a possibility of a place shared but where they aren't controlled; a place to dip in and out of when they can't cope with too much. This is why people say Renew spaces are so life-giving. A gradual return to family life. A finding of a new way of being family. A healing place when 'family' has not been a good word. No expectations, just acceptance.

There are lots of ways to be active in a family context, but this is my alphabet of wellbeing and Renew Wellbeing has been the best thing I have seen for healthy family connections – where family is redefined to include all. Your story will be different, but if you need something like this, why not set up a Renew space or share a simple meal, an encouraging word, a smile?

 Take Notice

Let me tell you the story of one little church in Nottingham at this point. New Life Baptist church[4] meets in a school hall, has a smallish, ageing congregation and is one of the best examples of family you could wish to be part of. Over the years, I was part of and then led this church; they have been through some bad times and some joyful times. There have been obstacles and miracles. But the beauty of this crowd is that they operate as family, not as a small religious business. I used to wonder if it was because they had no church building. I'm not sure. But for certain, there has always been a sense of deep love and compassion. Love for God, love for each other and love for others.

When I had a breakdown, they loved me back to health. Even though I talk about times when I couldn't be at church as people kept wanting to pat me and pray for me, it was all well-meant! Then when I had come back to some degree of health, these brave folk appointed me to lead them full-time, knowing full well I could break again and that my heart had been lost to those on the margins. They knew I would not be a leader to just keep them safe and comfortable, but they took the risk and with great grace they gave me space to grow.

They also kept open hearts to do whatever God was asking of them, including giving away all their reserves to inner city and overseas projects and then setting up an expensive place on the high street that many of them would never get to use, so that the most isolated could have a place to belong.

Even after I left to set up Renew Wellbeing as a national charity, they continued pouring out their time, love and finances to keep renew37 running four days a week. To see a project out-survive its founder and better still, to get stronger and better when the founder leaves, is a wonderful thing.

This church is family. I think every church is meant to be just that. Family is beyond blood.

Give

QUESTIONS

What images does the word 'family' bring up for you?

When have you experienced a good family?

What is missing for you in this area of family life, and can you bring it to God?

PRAYER

Father who holds us
Son who enfolds us
Spirit who gives love a voice
Teach us to love
Like you first loved us
To be deep-hearted family
Not as duty but choice

Resources

Will van der Hart, *The Power of Belonging*. Will, from the Mind and Soul Foundation,[5] draws from his experience in church leadership and the field of mental wellbeing to outline why belonging is so vital for our mental and emotional health.

G is for Growth

 **Connect**

The seed . . . grows; he knows not how. (Mark 4:27)

The choice of the word 'grow' or 'growth' here as a word associated with wellbeing will not come as a surprise.

I am no great gardener. I have dabbled a bit since having to be at home more and am grateful for our little patch of green. I've no idea what I'm doing, really, and yet things still grow. Granted, a lot of them are weeds, but pretty ones sometimes! It is wonderful to see things grow, isn't it?

The Bible uses the cultivation image a lot. God creates a garden at the beginning of time and walks in it 'in the cool of the day' (Gen. 3:8). Land was given to people as a blessing if it was fruitful and produced good growth (Exod. 3:17). In the Psalms we are told to be like trees planted by water (Ps. 1:3). Jesus talks about himself as a vine and believers as branches (John 15:5).

There is a lot of growing going on. I particularly love all the parables Jesus told about farmers and seed and soil and growth. There is so much to learn from them. A particular favourite is the one found in Mark 4 about the farmer who sows seed and then he wakes and sleeps and the seed grows and 'he knows not how' (v. 27). This story makes me smile as I have seen God grow me and grow the Renew charity and I have no idea how it happened. I have just attended to my rhythms and practices.

I wake and I sleep. There is such wonder when a plant appears above the ground, isn't there? As I write, it is the start of spring and I am amazed that despite zero skill and attention from me there is life popping up in my garden. Spring flowers and wildflowers and buds on the trees are appearing and I am doing nothing. In this instance you could say the plant is doing it all, but I wonder if they are just as amazed that they have survived another winter!

Growth starts under the ground. Off stage. The same has been true of growth in my own grasp of wellbeing practices and what *shalom* looks like. It is slow and practically invisible at times in my peace levels and actual life, but deep down in my soul God is at work. Every lesson learned, every season passed, every failure accepted, every cup offered brings a deeper root system into the soil of God's love for the little plant of my life. When eventually I see or feel *shalom*, peace, wellbeing, it can be a tiny green shoot that needs light and water, but weirdly, sometimes wellbeing can grow despite me, not because of me. It grows and I know not how. I did not see a deep fascination with wellbeing growing in me when I was lying in bed watching reruns of old TV shows in a darkened room because I couldn't cope with life, but the root system was growing. I did not see any growth in the early days of showing up and sitting in renew37 and colouring in and wondering if we had done the right thing, but the little green shoots were popping up. I did not see growth when I gave up the day job and the nice salary to set up this charity, but the new Renew spaces growing all over the UK were already

> Sometimes wellbeing can grow despite me, not because of me. It grows and I know not how.

beginning to multiply. The seed that God gave me of wellbeing practices born in dark days, when given back to him, has begun to produce fruit.

In my own life, the 'fruit of the Spirit', which is 'love, joy, peace, patience, kindness, goodness, faithfulness, gentleness and self-control' (Gal. 5:22,23), is not always showing, but when I submit to the growing process and the Spirit of God who makes growth happen, when I stay grafted onto the vine of Jesus himself, fruit can sometimes appear. Growth happens.

 Learn

Learning to weed and water

My daily habits of prayer and reading the Bible, meditation and slowing down to do something creative are a little like the weeding and watering that any growing plant needs.

If you are a gardener, you will know that daily weeding is needed in summer months or it all gets out of control. I worked that out the hard way. We have a pebble driveway at the back of our house that is a weed hotbed. I know that if I just go out each day and pull a few weeds, it won't get out of control. I know that if I see a weed and pull it up, it can look quite lovely out there. But I don't always do this.

A couple of years ago we decided the best way to tackle this large area of weeds was to lift all the stones from the drive, which is several metres long and a couple of metres wide. We painstakingly and back-breakingly spent many hours shovelling stones into wheelbarrows and putting them in enormous piles so that we could get to the bottom of what was happening with the weeds. To our surprise there was a weed membrane – a rotten old one, but there was one there! Most of the weeds we could see on the surface had rooted themselves above the weed membrane in the soil that had accumulated between the stones over years; these were not deep-rooted troublemakers. But over time, as we had left them, some had rooted right through the membrane to the soil below. This was a case of little seeds dropping on the surface and us not taking time to lift them out before they decided our driveway was a good home for them.

We replaced the weed membrane and all the stones. It took weeks. What I had learned was there was no big fix needed. Just lots of little moments. The weeds would still come as birds and wind dropped seeds on this newly cleared space. If I didn't want to have another month moving stones from one place to another, it was a simple constant task of pulling up a few weeds each day.

I know there are gardeners reading this and wondering when I get to the bit about weed killer. I haven't got there yet. I thought this way would be better for the environment. Maybe it's just a better visual lesson for me. I am an all or nothing person; I prefer a fix rather than a discipline. Gardening, particularly weeding, is teaching me how to look after my inner world better. Little and often. A psalm a week, a phrase a day, a rhythm of prayer, a hobby, some habits: this is the way to wellbeing for me.

> Gardening, particularly weeding, is teaching me how to look after my inner world better. Little and often.

 **Get Active**

Just a quick word here about shared green spaces.

There have been lots of occasions where we believe God has spoken to us at Renew Wellbeing about being an organic movement, of our centres being like allotments, each producing different vegetables and fruit but sharing tools and extra produce. There has always been a sense of a call to grow wellbeing – to plant seeds of wellbeing and let them grow. Renew spaces are like allotments, each with different soil and weather conditions, but the seed is the same. It is *shalom* and it holds the DNA of presence, partnership and prayer.

But growth is not seen in terms of numbers and size. There is growth in the small things, in the showing up, in the characters of those who attend. It is hard to measure, but it is fruitful.

Renew green spaces in Ruddington has just begun as I write these words. This village church has been running a Renew space in a café for several years, and in response to the need to stay outdoors to reduce coronavirus spread, they decided to set up Renew on an allotment. It is glorious and so simple. What a lovely thing to see the activities in a Renew space all centred around cultivation, when this has been such a strong image for the movement.

The prayer space is next to the shed with a circle of chairs. Signs explain what happens and when. Folk can join in the cultivation and then choose to pause and pray at the set prayer times if they wish.

Partnership with a local social prescribing agency[1] connected to the church is already strong.

This is a great idea. I am excited to see Renew green spaces pop up all over the place, alongside the indoor spaces.

 Take Notice

One of the pictures of growth that has impacted my thinking has come from some plants in my sister's garden on the Isle of Man. This is a beautiful walled garden with some well-established fruit trees that gives my brother-in-law plenty of fruit for his jam-making and furnishes us with great crumbles when we go to stay.

The strangest thing is that even though there are plenty of tall, well-formed fruit trees, the one that is always laden with fruit is the ugliest little stump of a tree you have ever seen. I would be tempted to use it for firewood had I not seen it weighed down with apples – so many that it is hard to use them all. Every little twisted branch is covered. The weird, leaning tree that looks close to death is actually the most fruitful.

Fruit can be produced in even the most insignificant-looking life.

The other lesson from the walled garden came a few years ago when they had to cut down a palm tree in the front garden and decided to take two cuttings for the back garden. My sister put one into an old chimney pot on the patio. It looked lovely. The other she placed in the long grass at the bottom of the garden.

A year later, I was astounded to see the difference in the two. The one in the pot still looked quite good. The same, really. But the one in the deep soil at the bottom of the garden was bigger than me. It continued to grow madly. Today, it still flourishes, while the one in the pot has long since died, as the soil it was in was shallow and needed more water than it ever received.

This lesson about growth needing deep roots, about good soil for the stuff you can't even see, has stuck with me. I had been so concerned with the visible life that I had not attended to the unseen. The roots.

I want to grow in my life. Even though it is 'OK not to be OK'. I want to be like Jesus more and more. No amount of forcing myself can do this; I need to be rooted in his love deeply, watered well with his Spirit, fed with his Word. Not pot-bound.

I know that however ordinary or even ugly I think my life is, the fruit can be remarkably tasty.

Give

QUESTIONS

What growing images are helpful to you and your wellbeing?

Have you tried gardening? How has that been for you?

What is helping you grow the roots deeper in your life?

PRAYER

The tools are out
The gardener is here
From empty tomb he has appeared
And clinging to
Your expert hands
Whilst doubts and questions may still stand

I will get active once again
Be thankful
That this gentle rain
Has filled the ground within my heart
With plants and weeds
And now before I start
I need to wait and listen
To the One who holds the seeds
To the gentle expert gardener
Who knows the wildflowers from the weeds

Resources

Muddy Church is a way of building worshipping communities outside around activities in the fresh air:

https://www.muddychurch.co.uk/

H is for Hope

 **Connect**

Hope does not disappoint . . . (Romans 5:5)

Hope is one of those words you would expect to find in a basket full of wellbeing words! We talk a lot about bringing hope and restoring hope and hoping for better days. Sometimes a familiar word loses its meaning in the overuse. I wondered whether to include this word at all. It was too obvious. But for me, hope is one of the big themes of wellbeing. Certainly when my wellbeing levels are low it is a sense of hopelessness that pervades.

Hope is used in the context of wishing for better things, better days, better health. But the Bible's concept of hope is much deeper and much richer.

When I was writing about growth I alluded to the fact that I am no gardener. One of the wonderful things, though, about my garden is that things grow there that I didn't even plant! Last year a whole load of beautiful forget-me-nots sprang up. I have never planted forget-me-nots. I'm not sure where they came from.

Hope feels like this at times. It is like something I didn't plant, but when it pops up in the garden of my soul, it is beautiful. God's hope and a sense of hopefulness is not something I feel I can cultivate, but it never ceases to amaze me how often hope is the dominant sensation I am left with after encountering God in any way.

The Bible talks of a 'hope [that] does not disappoint' us (Rom. 5:5, NRSV). This is the sort of hope we crave, right? Unfortunately, the context in the passage in Romans is that 'suffering produces endurance' which in turn 'produces character', which is what leads to hope that is not disappointing (vv. 3,4). Now, that's less attractive, isn't it? It seems that when we go through hard times, God is forming something in us – hope. It all smacks a little of my mum telling me things were character-building when they were things I didn't want to do!

> It seems that when we go through hard times, God is forming something in us – hope.

But the depth of this truth is different for me. When it comes to looking back over my wellbeing journey, it is in the most difficult times that the most character and hope is being formed. I remember writing in my journal part way through the terrible year of breakdown and voice loss after an encounter with God, 'I would rather have this intimacy with you, Lord, than get my voice and my life back.' This was a turning point in my recovery, not because God was trying to teach me something the hard way; I don't believe he is unkind like that. But this was the only way I could realize what was actually important in my life. God did not cause the suffering. I don't believe he ever does. He is all goodness. But he did show up in the darkness in such a way as to make me less afraid of my own vulnerability, more accepting of my own humanity. In short, he gave me hope.

This was not hope that I would get better, even, it was hope for hope's sake. Hope as a gift deep in my inner being. The Bible talks about faith being 'the assurance of things hoped for' (Heb. 11:1). Up to that dark point in my life, I had been hoping for so many things. I hoped I would please God, and please others. I hoped my children would be OK. I hoped we would all stay well. I suppose I hoped no one would notice the mismatch between my words and actions. I hoped a few people would come to faith. I hoped in things.

I now try to remember what I learned in those darker days and hope only for that which is certain. Putting all my hope in God himself, his goodness, his favour, his forgiveness, his kindness, his presence. This is a hope that can never disappoint. He never changes. Does that mean I am never disappointed? Well, obviously not! I have spoken and continue to speak honestly about my battle in prayer, my honest doubts, my love of the Psalms for their raw questioning of God. But the hope replanted in me on a daily basis as I practise the presence of 'the God of hope' (Rom. 15:13) is a divine gift, I believe.

This is why despair makes my heart hurt when I see it around me. It is the very opposite of the hope promised to us in Christ. When I felt despair myself, even though I was a Christian, it made no sense. Hope that doesn't disappoint is such a precious thing. My subsequent practices of inner wellbeing have all been about this sense of hope, if I'm honest. Practising the presence of God brings me into a place where the soil of my soul can accept the seed of hope.

> Practising the presence of God brings me into a place where the soil of my soul can accept the seed of hope.

Jeremiah 29:11 promises us a 'hope and a future' (NIV). This is at the heart of the wellbeing promised and offered to us in the gospel.

Learn

Praying with pictures of hope

For me, this learning about hope is an ongoing process. I am recognizing how much I am placing my hope in things other than God himself. There is daily work to be done in me as I spot where my hope has shifted from God himself to someone or something else.

For example, I place a lot of hope in my family being OK and doing well and being safe and making good choices. I have hopes for them and it can unsettle my peace massively when I feel these hopes are not being met.

A friend taught me how to pray for my children and those close to me without putting all my hope in the outcomes of their lives, or praying in a controlling way so that my hopes could be fulfilled in them. So now instead of begging God to sort one problem after another for my kids, I try to pray for them in this way.

First, I pray through Psalm 23 putting their name in as I pray: 'The LORD is . . .'s shepherd. They shall not want . . .' etc. In this way I am praying peace over them, whatever their choices. I also ask God for a visual image of each of the children.

For the eldest and his wife, I see eagles nesting in high places, waiting for thermals, soaring. As I pray, whatever their circumstances and need, I speak the truth of this image – that God will show them the thermals, that they will soar, not flap.

For the middle one and her partner, I see swans. It helps that I see swans every day on my walk. I see them gliding effortlessly on the water or waddling in an ungainly way on land, and

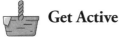

pray that my daughter and her partner would stay in the environment where they can glide. Once, during a tricky period in their lives, the swans on the river where I was praying took flight and their powerful, mighty wings took them upstream – which they could not have reached by gliding. I was able to pray that the hard time would take my daughter and her partner to a place that would be good for gliding again.

For the youngest, it is always a guide dog. I have always seen this picture of a faithful helper, and during the pandemic it was no surprise when he found himself using the hard circumstances of job uncertainty to become a carer.

As a mum, your influence shifts from guiding to praying as the children get older, and as a worrier I have embraced this way of praying to help me not interfere and fuss.

Hope rises in me for my children as I choose not to make them the subjects of my hope, but instead, to place my hope in God's faithfulness and kindness.

Get Active

As I write this, we are part of a national campaign that is helping to raise funds for churches who are bringing hope to communities through the pandemic.

It is being recognized at the highest levels of government that the local church is a hope-giving community.[1] There have been many, many stories over the years of churches getting stuck in and bringing hope to others.

The church has not been the only source of hope by any means, but it still thrills me that the 50,200 local churches in this nation can be at the very heart of bringing hope back to hopeless lives just by showing up and being kind.

People have had their hopes dashed in so many ways during the pandemic. Hopes of jobs, relationships or long lives, or promotions and holidays. Hopes of operations that would save lives, hopes of new places to live. Hope has been so badly affected that it will take a long time to recover these natural hopes. In the meantime, the church brings an offer of a hope not dependent on anything changeable. A hope that is strong and unwavering. A hope based in eternity.

And that hope can look like spaces we can share together to recover in. It looks like foods banks and housing projects and job clubs and counselling services.

But beyond all this, it looks like Jesus himself, living and breathing through his people with arms open to all who have had their hopes dashed, inviting them to put their hope in him.

 Take Notice

A new friend I made during lockdown has taught me so much about hope. At a low point when I was complaining about how hard it was to have hope when people you were praying for were dying, she told me her remarkable story of hope. Her book *Hope is Coming*[2] is a great read, but here are a few words especially written for this chapter. Thanks, Louise.

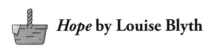
Hope by Louise Blyth

I used to measure hope in earthly realms. Hope was success at work, fun with friends and family, holidays and home improvements. I looked at life as some sort of to-do list which I purposefully navigated my heart towards. Hope used to be wrapped around the people I loved and the things I thought I should have. But then, just as we had the world at our feet, our lives were turned upside down in an instant. My 33-year-old husband was diagnosed with advanced bowel cancer. How could this be? This wasn't in the plan! As I cradled our babies and looked into his terrified eyes, hope was ripped out of our souls in that grey hospital room as seemingly everything we had based our lives around was mercilessly taken from us. As the days and months passed, we gently began to reframe our hope around treatment options, everyday joy and the very act of living itself. But even that type of hope wasn't enough when we got to the worst of the worse-case scenarios. Death began to loom for him in a way it never had before, and hope felt impossible when we looked into the eyes of the end of his life.

But then something remarkable happened.

I felt so hopeless that I screamed and begged God to show himself. I cried and voraciously told the big guy that 'it was now or never' for him to prove his existence to me.

What happened next was remarkable and miraculous. Hope flooded into every part of his body and his hospital room as we sat around his deathbed. Hope made us feel known, loved and joyful in the most painful and tragic of times. This was a different type of hope – I knew it but didn't know it, I couldn't touch it or show it to others. But I could feel it and my dying husband could feel it too. This hope transformed his death and my grief. It's a hope that's not of this world and yet is available to us all. It's a hope that no disease, no tragedy and no set of circumstances can take away from me. It's my God-given hope and it makes my own life as a young widow worth living and my own death worth awaiting. Hope is there for all of us, you just have to ask and let your heart show you the way.

Give

QUESTIONS

What are you hoping for now?

Can you name some things you put your hope in that may disappoint you?

Do you have any particular habits that help you place your hope in God (e.g. my prayer images when praying for my kids)?

Have you ever felt hope despite it being a very difficult time?

PRAYER

Take heart you shout
To fearful followers
Buffeted by storms
You water walking come
To calm them
Knowing even storms
Can't harm them
Calling out across the waves
You shout
Take heart

Take heart
You say
To those who dare
To step out of the
Safety zone
Believe
You are the
Way back home
Then panic
falter, sink and cry
Lord why?
Save me I pray
And reaching out you say
Take heart!

Take heart
You whisper in the boat
That now unhindered
By the storms
You calmed[3]
Can simply float
And presence of the One revealed
Our peace, our joy, our hope is sealed
I hear you whisper in my ear
So near
Take heart

So take my heart
It's yours
I don't know fully who you are
But in this fresh calm pause
I do believe
I will believe
You are the very air I breathe
And now with taken heart
My day can really start

And taking heart
I see my moments differently
And joy
A sharpened surgeon's knife
Begins to shape my soul, my life.

Take joy
Take hope
Be whole
Bless the Lord, bless the Lord, O my soul[4]

Resources

Louise Blyth, *Hope is Coming*.

I is for Interests

 **Connect**

We are God's masterpiece. (Ephesians 2:10, NLT)

This is a less obvious word to pick, I suppose. Interests. It's not a great wellbeing word like 'compassion' or 'joy', is it? But this idea that we all have interests, hobbies or strengths is vital for wellbeing, I think. When I became unwell I had forgotten to take time to play, to enjoy hobbies, simply to be. It was one of the things I needed help from my community with and is at the heart of a Renew space – shared interests or hobbies.

But why do I think this is a deep issue in God's heart too? Isn't it a waste of time doing creative things when there is a world to be saved? I had certainly been brought up with loads of creativity around me. We always had 'projects' on the go. I remember making a Cluedo game out of old boxes and toilet roll tubes with my sisters, and sewing the entire cast of Winnie the Pooh from old curtains. Yet as I got older, the serious message of salvation separated itself from more frivolous human recreation. I always chose to spend my time on that which, I was told, would have eternal value. I was rarely told that would be crochet!

What I had failed to notice in my study of the Word of God was how very creative and playful he is. Reading again the Genesis account of creation, I now meet a God who loves to make stuff. Who takes delight in creativity. Working my way through the Gospels I meet with a Saviour who loved to take time over meals, who attended weddings, who spent years prior to public ministry carving wood, who hung out with fishermen and cooked up a great beach breakfast.

Looking at one of my favourite verses in Ephesians, 'We are God's masterpiece. He has created us anew in Christ Jesus, so we can do the good things he planned for us long ago' (2:10, NLT), I meet with a God who loved creating us, all different, all unique. He made us as we are, on purpose. His creation shows great attention to detail, great love and care. I would even say it shows great enjoyment.

But not only does it say here that he made us on purpose, it also says he made us *for* purpose. He made us each with gifts and skills that he planned 'in advance for us' (NIV), good things for us to do.

To have something to do is vital for our wellbeing. I know not everyone can do paid work, but everyone has some unique and inherent value that they bring to the world. Those unable to outwork that because of physical limitations bring joy and meaning in other ways. For most of us, there are things that we get great pleasure from doing, a great sense of satisfaction from creating. We are made in our Father's image (Gen. 1:27). Our heavenly Father, creator of all things.

So to make, to do, to craft, to enjoy hobbies and activity, to have interests is to express something of the One we were made to represent. It is a spiritual activity to do something creative, to work, to engage in a hobby. The separation between sacred and secular, worldly and spiritual exists only in our dualistic minds, not in God's holistic plan.

Our interests are part of what makes us his masterpiece under construction. We are his project; he made and is making us. As a reflection of that deep truth, we find ourselves as creators and makers of things that he has given us to watch over and care for.

Our interests are part of what makes us his masterpiece under construction.

 Learn

Pick a hobby – any hobby

One of the key practices for my wellbeing is attending to my interests, my hobbies, the things that bring me life. For each of us, these things will be very different, so my sharing here what works for me will only be by way of invitation for you to explore this letter for yourself.

I love the outdoors and find myself close to God when I am close to vast expanses of water. In fact, I can't be near water without getting in it. Well, not always . . . I have managed to cross the Irish Sea and the Channel quite a few times without being tempted to jump off the ferry! But when I go to the beach, which is one of my best 'happy' places, unless it is deepest winter, I just can't resist a dip. I love mountain streams and valleys with rivers. There have been times when my poor family have been held up on a walk because I just had to jump in a plunge pool and then borrow spare clothes to get back to the car. On one of these walks as I stripped down to what I felt was a decent amount of clothes to still have something dry left for getting home, my eldest son was heard to say, 'Mum, have a bit of respect. Grandad's here!' As if my poor old dad wasn't used to my obsession with a wild swim!

But living as I have in land-locked Nottingham for the last three decades plus, I have needed to find other life-giving pursuits too. I am what my other son calls a 'crochet-aholic', by which he means I crochet constantly. I'm not even that keen on the end products, I just find the repetitive process of stitch after stitch very calming. I find this particularly helpful when on a long car journey; I am a nervous passenger. We have some mammoth crocheted blankets from our family holidays. I also love painting stones, trying out calligraphy, reading almost anything and I love language-learning (hence seeing wellbeing as a language, I suppose).

I loved every day of teaching – well, not every day maybe, but most of them! I loved seeing children learn to read, and shine and value themselves and others. I love spending time with my family. This has been the worst part of this pandemic at the time of writing, the separation from loved ones. Just hanging out together is enough to put a spring back in my step.

Some of these hobbies are unique to me, some can be done with others, but all make me feel more alive. I am still me without them, but life has less flavour.

To engage fully with an interest, to lose yourself in it, is part of being human and good for your wellbeing. It is not an added extra, but an essential ingredient deserving of time and space in the diary.

 **Get Active**

Some of these interests can be engaged in, in a shared space, and that is what is at the heart of our Renew spaces. It is quite simply an invitation to bring what you might be doing at home for your wellbeing and do it together. To bring a spare for a friend. Not all hobbies and interests lend themselves to this – I can't easily wild swim in a café space. But I can bring my stone painting.

But why would I? Surely our hobbies are personal to us and often help us escape from others? Yes, of course we need our time alone but having realized how many folk were lonely, were spending all day without anyone to talk to, I wondered if it might be good to just be together and take the pressure off the conversation by having things to do. This has proved to be the case. It is great to spend time with others companionably, getting on with what we have brought or what is on offer and sometimes chatting, sometimes not. There is something so beautiful about a space where each person is celebrating their uniqueness, not just coming to be fixed. Renew wellbeing is a strength-based approach to community, and as such we encourage each person to share a hobby or interest. In this way we can learn new skills, see people in a new light, and renew wellbeing in the area of accepting ourselves and others for who we are, not just what our label is.

> There is something so beautiful about a space where each person is celebrating their uniqueness, not just coming to be fixed.

 **Take Notice**

Let me take you on a little tour round a Renew space.

As you come through the door, there are a few folk just sitting watching the world go by in the front window. They don't seem to have any activities going on and nobody is forcing them to join in. It seems enough that they got through the door. One man still has his coat on and is cradling a cup of coffee like a shield against unwanted socializing. The table directly in front of the door is big, with about eight people gathered round chatting, and it seems there are about three hobbies going on here. One lady is mounting her photos taken on holiday onto cards to sell in support of the local homeless hostel. Every now and then, she asks the opinion of the people sitting in the window about which one to choose. They all have strong opinions. A few people at this table are being led by a lady in learning to make origami boxes. It looks very complex and everyone is very quiet, concentrating hard, until one lady laughs and the table dissolves at her attempt as she crumples it up and starts again. It turns out this lady is one of the hosts, the organizers, but it would have been hard to tell who's who. No one seems too bothered about the outcome. Failure does seem to be a very real option.

Across the room, two men play dominoes at a table where two other folk are having a go at a crossword. In the corner, someone is fixing a broken shelf and someone else is making another round of drinks. The atmosphere is calm and quiet apart from the odd peal of laughter from the origami makers.

I sit down and am handed some knitting needles by the lady next to me, who asks if I want to knit a penguin jumper or a hat for a bottle. She assures me it's all for charity and I am intrigued. When I tell her I can't knit, she calmly sets about teaching me. She looks thrilled to be able to show someone what she is obviously brilliant at. I'm not sure my attempt will make it to a penguin or even a bottle, but I enjoy the time quietly talking about knitting with this lady. She tells me she pops in every day and it gives her a reason to get out of bed. She tells me this place is more like home than her home is. She makes me want to cry.

Give

QUESTIONS

What hobbies or interests give you life?

Why do you sometimes forget to prioritize doing these things?

Which of these could you share with others in a shared space?

If you couldn't think of any hobbies, what interests you? What might you like to learn?

PRAYER

God of the detail
God of all things
Creator
Designer
From weevils to wings
Remind me
You made me
On purpose
As me
With gifts and with interests
Please help me just be
Myself
Image bearer
Of the One who is here
I choose life in the small things
In my interests you're near

Resources

I love the craft course run by 'Peaced Together':
www.peacedtogether.co.uk

Check out the list of activities for wellbeing on:
www.mind.org.uk

J is for Joy

 **Connect**

The joy of the LORD is your strength. (Nehemiah 8:10)

'Joy' is something you would expect to find in a list of important wellbeing words, especially if you were brought up on joyful Sunday school songs like me.

As I look with the beauty of hindsight at the teaching about joy from the Bible, I do question whether I have ever understood the word.

'The joy of the LORD is your strength' was used as a rabble-rouser in meetings to make sure we left looking happy. 'Joy' and 'happiness' were often interchanged and used to speak of the same thing. I am now convinced they are not the same at all.

In Hebrew, the word used here is from the word '*chadah*', which means to be made joyful; it is used in celebrations and feasts. It seems to be less a feeling and more of an act of the will, as I understand it. The celebrations of the Old Testament were many and were part of remembering the story of who people were and what God had done. In the New Testament, we are told that joy is a fruit of the Holy Spirit in our lives. He brings the fruit, we are just branches for the fruit to grow on. We can't make it happen. We can't push the fruit of joy out by being jollier. The

> We can't push the fruit of joy out by being jollier.

Greek word here is '*chairo*' – to be glad, rejoice. Again, this is a verb. Something is being done here when joy is announced. It looks like something. And here God is the giver of joy, the One who is joy in us.

The Bible talks about Jesus going to the cross for the 'joy . . . set before him' (Heb. 12:2). I don't imagine for one minute Jesus, who is fully God, fully man, was happy about the cross and its suffering, but the joy 'set before him', I believe, was union with us, with his creation, with his precious ones. This knowledge that he would be able to rejoice with us because he beat death and hell, this joy was enough to take him all the way to the cross and beyond. I am not convinced a happy thought would do this. Joy is deeper.

Happy as an English word comes from the root that implies good luck and fortunate circumstances. Joy is from the Latin meaning to rejoice or take pleasure in. It is less a transient feeling dependent on circumstances and more a definite act of the will because of a bigger story.

As I am coming to understand joy I see it, or rather hear it, as a deep bass note to my life. The melody might be a jig or a lament, but the bass note is steady because it is the work of the Spirit of God in me. It is 'love, joy, peace, patience, kindness, goodness, faithfulness, gentleness, self-control' (Gal. 5:22,23). So those of you who know me might struggle to hear the bass line at times as the melody shouts above it, but if joy is one of the fruits of the presence of God in my life, then it is not dependent on what I feel or the tune I sing but on his character. The 'joy of the LORD', which is my strength, which is a verb, is more of his doing than mine. I join in by dwelling in his presence more and more. Joy can co-exist with pain and sadness. Happiness seems unable to. Joy can be there even when we can't feel it. Happiness comes and goes with our situation in life. Joy strengthens us even in the more minor key moments; happiness evades us more than it finds us. Joy is the free gift of a loving Father to all equally. I'm a fan of the word 'joy', in case you hadn't noticed, and less of a fan of the word 'happiness', although I know many people who have greater knowledge than me who would argue just as powerfully for the word 'happiness'. As for me, I am pursuing joy.

> Joy can co-exist with pain and sadness.

 Learn

Press pause in ordinary moments

So, how do I pursue joy without giving into relentless positivity that can tend towards dishonesty if I'm not careful?

What joyful habits do I have?

Joy seeps in when I engage in ordinary tasks if I take time to pause. Here is a habit that is so simple I nearly missed it out when I was planning this book. It is the habit of pause. It is not the same as sitting still or meditating or mindfulness. It is so much simpler that I almost don't notice it. But I notice when I don't do it! The habit is to press pause.

This is something I am very familiar with when watching TV. The way we now watch is rarely in real time. We usually watch pre-recorded things or programmes we can pause online. We frequently find ourselves needing a cuppa or a snack, there's someone at the door, or the phone rings and without pause we would miss something.

As I am so adept at using pause for my leisure viewing, it is amazing how hard I find it in my everyday life.

You see, if we don't press pause in a moment, we may miss something good. Making a cup of fresh coffee. Pause. Hearing my children or a good friend or family member on the phone. Pause. Taking my dog for a walk or having a Netflix night in with my husband. Pause.

The pause can lead to a reflection, mindfulness or meditation, but sometimes it is as simple as having a brief moment to take in what we are actually feeling and to let joy seep in. Often this happens alongside pain or sadness, but there is still room for a little moment of joy. We can feel like there will be no joy until all the pain has gone, but the pause helps me hear the deep bass note regardless of what the melody sounds like.

The other day I looked up from my desk and saw a murmuration of starlings right outside my window. Pause. I find joy in every rainbow and every sunset and have determined since my recovery to pause if possible if I ever see one, and enjoy it. It was my illness that gave me the time to realize I was missing out on joy in the little things by constantly worrying and rushing on to the next thing.

Learning to press pause is becoming a vital part of my wellbeing, as I am such an activist still. I am usually thinking of the next thing while doing the current thing. It makes me rush. It makes me miss the joy if I'm not careful.

 **Get Active**

Margaret, one of our coordinators, has been the queen of the online platform Zoom during lockdown, and the joy of small activities on screens has been wonderful to hear about.

Margaret writes:

So 'Joy' – in lockdown that would be the fun and laughter we have shared doing all sorts of random online quizzes, like working out brands, films and songs written as emoticons, or trying to guess the object from a microscope image.

Joy in normal circumstances – seeing two very different characters playing dominoes together and discovering common likes and dislikes, laughing together and building friendship.

Here is Margaret's advice for running a Renew Zoom (i.e. a Renew space online):

Set up a Zoom link using the guidelines available on the website. Decide whether using the same link, or whether using a different link each week, is safest in your particular context.

Invite others to join you. This is a good opportunity to reach out to those on the margins of church life. I send a link to the church list every week, along with others who I know are keen to join us.

Invite people to bring a hobby and a drink with them.

Chat about one another's hobbies and any activities people may have enjoyed during the week. I also find that the Table Talk for Wellbeing – The Ugly Duckling Company Shop (uglyducklingresources.org) are a really useful resource to help conversation flow.

You can set up a PowerPoint with quizzes on. Place the quizzes to the left of the screen as people's Zoom screens will come up on the right. You can use the annotate facility (top bar) on Zoom to do word searches, spot the difference, crosswords, Sudoku etc., but be aware that anyone using a small screen will find this tricky.

Emoji and logo quizzes work well as PowerPoints and/or are available online.

There are numerous online quizzes. I pick a theme each week and then google for quizzes – e.g., 'Spring Quiz' in google search. If sharing videos remember to click the two squares on the screen after you have clicked screen share – 'share sound' and 'optimize video'.

'Name the object' quiz is another idea – google for several possibilities.

PRAYER. Remember to make it clear when you plan to pray and ensure that you are giving people space and permission to choose whether or not to participate.

Templates for prayer are available in the Renew Wellbeing resources, as are PowerPoints to help you lead. Renewwellbeing.org.uk.

 Take Notice

Here is a thing that brings me so much joy.

On Easter Monday every year, I love to re-enact the most fantastic bit of the Easter story that always brings me joy.

The part in John 21 where Jesus cooks his friends a beach breakfast fills my heart with joy. Here is the risen Christ. He has been to hell and back. But now here he is, with a barbecue on a beach. Not what most of us would do. But he knows how weary and sad his followers have been. He knows how disappointed with himself Peter is. He knows they have been fishing all night and caught nothing and so he makes a fire and cooks fish and bread. The disciples must have been amazed, thrilled, awestruck. Breakfast on the beach with the risen Christ.

Whenever I am in the Isle of Man at Easter, regardless of the weather and the complaints from my poor family, I have taken blankets and disposable barbecues and Manx kippers and headed off to a windy stretch of coastline to battle the elements to bring a recreation of the moment to my dear family. Even if they don't appreciate it!

I know the Isle of Man is a slightly different climate to the land that Jesus walked, but we have had some lovely moments in amongst the freezing ones.

And every year it makes me amazed that this is who we follow. This One who makes breakfast. This One who knows us so well. This One who meets us in our need with simple things.

Whatever my family think (and to be honest, I think they love it really) I will still cook fish on an open fire (and sausage and bacon in an inappropriate departure from Jesus' practices!) whenever I can on Easter Monday each year because it brings me such joy.

Give

QUESTIONS

What brings you joy?

What do you think is the difference between joy and happiness?

Can you think of a time when joy and sorrow both existed together in your heart?

PRAYER

Based on Matthew 10:29

He never forgets a sparrow
He numbers the hairs on your head
It's God, not the devil, in details
From my first infant breath till I'm dead
It's him that has formed these features
It's him chose this mouth and this nose
It's his loving gaze every one of my days
He has watched over this frame as it grows

It's him made my internal organs
He sculpted my brain, breathed my soul
His tears mingle with mine when I'm hurt
It's his love fills my heart, makes me whole

If he made every feather and wing out there
And knows every sparrow we see
I don't need to fear
Fret the small stuff
His attention to detail's for me

See me, Lord
Know my heart
Have this breath
Help me start
Again

Today
To trust
Just you

Fix my gaze on what is good and true

God of the sparrow
Hair-counting friend
You hold me all day
From beginning to end

Resources

The Happiness Lab by Ugly Duckling Company is a course with videos following several people as they try out different habits for their wellbeing and happiness: https://www.theuglyducklingcompany.com/thl

K is for Kindness

 **Connect**

The fruit of the Spirit is love, joy, peace, patience, kindness . . .
(Galatians 5:22, my emphasis)

Kindness is what love looks like. In the Hebrew the word
'*chesed*', which is translated 'loving kindness', can be found
twenty-three times in the Psalms alone. Two hundred and fifty
times in the Old Testament the word '*chesed*' is used. It is inte-
gral to God's character. It is more than kindness.

Chesed or loving kindness is a quality that involves faithfulness and deep love that acts on behalf of the recipient. It looks
like something in practice. I have often said that love in our
Renew centres looks like kindness. It is all well and good saying 'you love each other', but acts of kindness show that love.
Kindness is the way we know we are loved.

It is God's kindness towards us that we
see in the life, death and resurrection of
Jesus – his love in practice. Our love for
each other as humans is difficult to quan-
tify until we start being kind. When anyone is kind to another person they are
showing God's love, God's character.

> Kindness is
> underrated. A
> kind word, a
> kind act, a kind
> look can change
> a day.

Kindness is underrated. A kind word, a kind act, a kind look can change a day.

The Bible speaks a lot about God's kindness to us, but it also talks about kindness being the best way for us to be human together. Jesus, in Luke 6:31, tells us to treat others as we would like to be treated. In Colossians 3:12 we are told to clothe ourselves in kindness. I love this image of getting dressed in kindness, which is a translation of the Greek word '*chrestos*', which also means useful and good. I think that both Hebrew and Greek words translated as 'kind' or 'loving kindness' seem to imply some sort of action or activity. So we are encouraged to get dressed in kindness, in actually doing something kind for others.

In this language of wellbeing, this is one of the most important words for me because it is where 'the rubber hits the road'. This is where we can no longer talk about wellbeing and love and peace, but it actually has to look like something. This is where the gospel is so fantastic as the bigger story in which I am held. It is not a set of beliefs in a distant God who would like me to be a bit nicer, but a life founded on the kindness of God who gave his own life for mine. I am wanting to get to the point where I don't need God to keep proving his kindness and then doubting he is kind every time a prayer goes unanswered. As I consider what he has already done in creating me and then coming to be one of us and dying and rising again to beat death and hell and give me life, I know he is kind. Any other evidence that suggests he isn't must remain a mystery. I am trying to hold onto the timeless act of kindness that is the Easter story.

Learn

Learning to get yourself dressed first

I refer here to kindness being something you can clothe your-self in, as Paul talks about in Colossians 3:12. So let's look at something I hope we all do every day as a help to practising kindness. Getting dressed. On a good day, choosing what to wear and putting it on makes me think of what God clothes me in. In a sense I am getting ready inside as well as outside for the day. On a bad day I may as well stay in my pyjamas!

I used to start the day thinking of all the people I needed to be kind to, listing what needed to be done so I could be Christ-like to others. There is nothing wrong with this but, for me, it is a bit like getting everyone else dressed and not dressing myself first. To be kind to others involves receiving kindness, being kind to myself. Kindness is not a duty but an overflow.

So this section seems a little unnecessary, doesn't it? What are my practices of kindness? Well, they are exactly that . . . being kind in small ways to myself, and to others. Kind words, kind actions. Some days are better than others.

So, I will share with you here what I am learning about the good and bad days with my kindness journey. On a good day I start the day knowing I am held by a kind God. I use morn-ing prayer to list the ways God has showed me his kindness in Christ, in creation, in the love of those around me. I end the day reviewing all the kindness I have seen and so I start the next day looking for kindness. On a good day I allow his kind-ness to fill me so it overflows a bit at times, and I find myself responding to the inner prompt to send that word of encouragement, to leave those flowers, to ring that friend.

On a bad day I fail to sit with God and know his kind hands around me. I start the day recounting when I have been offended and hurt, and amongst the complaints I don't even look for signs of God's kindness. I quickly believe the evidence of my eyes that God must no longer love me, no longer be kind. I speak unkind words about myself in my head and then unsurprisingly I don't exactly overflow with kindness to others, preferring to keep myself to myself. I don't review the day and if I do, it is only to look for evidence that God and others have been unkind.

But the wonder of the good and bad days is this. God doesn't love me any less on the bad days. He is kindness. He is *chesed*. I am loved with everlasting kindness and so I can start again the next day. I can take up my cup again the next day and start fresh. The beauty of this view of being held in kindness, not just trying hard to be kind, is that God lays out the clothes for us washed fresh each day and ready to put on again. So, we can be ready to clothe ourselves in kindness even if we had a grumpy, kindness-free day the day before.

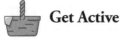 **Get Active**

In community this is one of those letters that is easy to see. Kindness is the flavour of a good community wellbeing space. A good Renew space, or indeed, any community space or group determined to show love, is a wonderful learning ground for how to be kind. It isn't that this will be easy. It will be easier to stay away from community. It will be easier to criticize and complain. It will be easier to take offence. But God puts us in families, in communities, to have somewhere to practise being kind. Even when we don't feel like it.

There is something about seeing kindness in operation that makes you want to join in. I have a dream of every church in the land having a space where they just practise kindness every day. I suppose that is what is at the heart of the Renew dream. Kindness is creative and rich; there are many and varied ways to be kind, and it makes you feel good to do it.

Some examples I have heard of kindness in action in our Renew spaces include these:

One of our regulars was really sad one day and another regular as well as offering kind words gave away the painting they had been working on for ages to help the person feeling sad to know they were loved.

One regular found that she had loads of craft supplies at home from a previous job and brought in a different activity every week, giving her time and resources freely to anyone wanting to learn a new skill.

One of our regulars brought extra produce regularly from his allotment and shared it with anyone at the centre.

The regulars at our space always put a little do together for anyone having a birthday. It brings such joy.

One of our regulars used his skills to build us loads of planters for outside our space. He gave us his time and the wood freely.

When anyone is feeling down at our place, it is rarely the hosts who end up helping in any way. It is usually another regular who offers a word of comfort or wisdom from their own story.

 Take Notice

Many years ago, when our three children were small and my husband, Mark, and I were living squashed together with them in a two-bedroom end terrace, struggling to make ends meet due to lifestyle changes, I experienced real kindness and it changed us all.

Don't get me wrong, we have a supportive family on both sides. We are so fortunate. But we had decided on job changes that meant that money was really tight, and we didn't want to keep bothering our families to help us. It was embarrassing, to say the least.

We were also part of an amazingly kind church. Kindness was a big value and when each of the children were born we didn't have to make our own meals for weeks at a time. I should have carried on having children, really!

But there are times in our lives when we feel we should bear the consequences of our own decisions and find it hard to ask for help. Any number of family or friends would have helped us if we had asked. But this particular time in our lives, money was a bit thin on the ground. Every penny was accounted for and Christmas was coming. There were three children with massive expectations after watching too many TV adverts with shiny things, and a frantic mother with an empty purse.

This is not a tale of real poverty. These children would not go hungry; our families would be buying them plenty of stuff.

Others have it so much worse, I know. But I am a big fan of celebrations and gifts and occasions. I love to wrap things up. Even if they aren't expensive or even wanted . . . I love gift-giving.

So, to be approaching a sparse Christmas with a houseful of small people was filling me with anxiety. I wanted to be able to give them something. Mark worried less than me, but we were both feeling the pinch that year.

To make matters worse, I was working late shifts at a large toy store for an hourly pittance and watching other parents load their trolleys with things I couldn't buy for my children. They didn't need all these things. But it was me that was struggling.

I cried out to God one night about it. This was back in the days before my breakdown, when I felt there was a right and wrong way to pray, so even as I was asking God for help I was berating myself for even asking when there were people in the world so much worse off than us.

So it was with great surprise that I opened the door to a stranger the next day who was walking away, having deposited three big bin liners on my doorstep. I called after him, a bit confused, to be told they were gifts from God. Then the man got in his car and drove away, leaving me standing there with my mouth open.

Each of the three large bags contained enough gifts for each of our children, appropriate to their age. Beautiful things, funny things, unusual things. All the things I would have bought if we could have afforded it.

As the tears flowed I realized I didn't know who to thank. How could I receive these? Then I remembered his words. They were a gift from God. So I began to thank God and quickly hide the bags to wrap these God-given goodies, ready for Christmas. I have told my children since that this is their story. It was not our generosity and kindness that year that made Christmas for them, it was God's and the stranger who listened to God's voice.

If you are that stranger or any other kind stranger who has given gifts and love to others without knowing why, thank you for your kindness. It changed my world view and my heart that day. Kindness is part of my children's vocabulary because of moments like that. The kindness of God that looks like something.

Give

QUESTIONS

When have you been the recipient of a kind act? How did it feel?

What is the kindest moment you can think of?

Could you think of one kind act or word of kindness to give today, and actually do it?

PRAYER

How kind you are
O Lord of my heart
Your kindness
Won't stop
And I can't see the start

I was born by your kindness
And kept by your love
And the kind
Acts of others
Keep my eyes fixed above

Resources

Kindness Day UK encourages everyone to work towards a day of kindness a year. I would suggest using their ideas every day: https://www.kindnessuk.com/world_kindness_day_kindness_day_uk.php

L is for Lament

 **Connect**

How long, O LORD? (Psalm 13:1)

This may seem like a bit of a depressing word to bring into an alphabet of wellbeing. Lament is to be able to express grief and sorrow. The Psalms are full of lament, outpourings of sadness and loss. It may not seem like a good thing to encourage people to lament or moan for their wellbeing, but I have found this to be a vital part of my wellbeing journey. To be able to acknowledge and express negative emotion, not just the jollies.

> I have found this to be a vital part of my wellbeing journey. To be able to acknowledge and express negative emotion.

This morning my Gospel reading (I like to read a bit of one of the Gospels each day so I can learn from Jesus constantly) was in Luke 19 where Jesus expresses lots of negative emotion. We see him weeping over Jerusalem with sorrow and then getting angry enough at people misusing the temple to start turning over tables. This is a picture of God in human form fully engaged with lament.

There is a whole book of the Bible called Lamentations. So lament is obviously a key element to being human.

It is the Psalms that draw my focus, though. Before I was unwell I had enjoyed the odd psalm of praise and found the others a bit confusing and depressing. Was it really OK to ask God to break someone's teeth?[1] Many psalms contain lament and praise. The psalm writers seemed to be able to leap from one emotion to another and still call it prayer. From the time I experienced burnout onwards, the Psalms became great friends to me. I could always settle myself within one of the spaces the Psalms made with their mix of words. I could always find an example of prayer being less polished and more negative than I had thought it should be. In the Psalms I learned that it is 'OK not to be OK'; that prayer is acceptable to God even when it is a groan.

For each person to be the one who best knows their own heart, or to come to know the One who best knows our hearts, can lead us to the best sort of therapy. For me, that has been an ability to find expression for sadness, loss and negative emotion.

 Learn

Learning to journal the ups and the downs

The practice of journaling has allowed me to pour out what I am feeling without judgement onto a page. By journaling I do not mean a 'Dear Diary' approach. I don't write every day and I don't write everything. Sometimes I doodle or draw (badly), sometimes I write letters to God, sometimes lists. Sometimes I write one word on a page and just look at it. It is between me and God. Not for public consumption! This is where my daily habit with meditation on the Psalms has been so vital. It has informed my journaling to the point where I dare to call some of the things I write 'my psalms'. I love the Psalms and read them daily. The origin of the word 'psalm' is, however, to do with praise. So it seems strange to be using the word in the context of honest expression of emotion, even negative emotion. Can that be praise?

In my practice of the presence of God,[2] in my relationship with God, it is an expression of faith to pour out all that is within me, not just the shiny, positive stuff. This is an act of praise for me as I recognize that there is a God who cares for me, and try to hold nothing back as I stand before him. To acknowledge who he is and still wail at the state of the world, my own life, or some mystery that makes me doubt his goodness: this is all part of the rich tapestry of lament and praise that is prayer. This is what I find so eloquently in the Psalms. This is what has invited me into a language that is not as polite as it used to be when I pray and spend time with God.

To have permission to bring 'all that is within me' (Ps. 103:1) as I encourage my own soul to bless his name each day, means I have to be honest about that which is in me that is not beautiful or full of praise. To give voice to complaint and doubt and fear and sadness enables me to stand honestly in the presence of the One who knew all that was in there anyway.

> To give voice to complaint and doubt and fear and sadness enables me to stand honestly in the presence of the One who knew all that was in there anyway.

As a personal practice, using laments written by others – like the psalmists – can also be helpful, as at the times of deepest sadness we sometimes lose our own words.

When I was leading church full-time, I ended up taking funerals for those in our community who had no one to help them at times of crisis. It was such a privilege. It was always a psalm I ended up sharing with those grappling with loss. I began to realize how beautiful it can be to sit honestly and express grief or 'weep with those who weep' (Rom. 12:15). So often our own words feel hollow and empty in these times, so either silence or ancient words like the words of Scripture can be better.

 Get Active

To lament and allow for lament in community is not something we are usually comfortable with. If someone in our group expresses deep sorrow or negative emotion our tendency, my tendency, is to try to make that better. This is a natural human response. I spent many years avoiding other people's negatives as I really had no idea what to do with them. At the same time, perhaps unsurprisingly, I was burying my own negatives and trying to sing over them. The tradition I was part of over these years led me to have only one answer for anything that seemed wrong or broken – pray for it and make it go away. I still believe in a God who heals, but there have been times when I have pushed people away from the God they needed most because of my relentless positivity and need to fix everyone.

Having been in a dark place myself I realized that sometimes what I needed was not for people to listen to my problems and offer answers, but just to be heard and allowed to give voice to a genuine struggle and have it land in a shared space to be held by all. Often shared silence, a sigh, a quiet blessing, a hug or a hand on the shoulder was all I needed. I needed space to not be OK and a place to work that through in community, without making others feel in a panic that they had to sort me out.

After my recovery, I spent a few years trying to do the opposite of what I knew was needed. I tried running round being everyone's saviour. Unsurprisingly, that was not sustainable. I have heard it said that the church should be like a hospital. I am not at all sure about this. I don't think the local church can be the fourth emergency service. I'm just not sure we have the right staff! Not in the area of mental and emotional health. I am not convinced that our shared life is there so we can sort out each other's sadness and problems. I am increasingly convinced, though, of the value of shared spaces where sadness can exist and be held.

I loved the fact that when we opened renew37 I had a place where, even as the church leader, I could some days be far less than bouncy. This was a place where there were often no answers. I had learned from taking many funerals that what people in pain want is not a glib response, but just company to sit in the dark. Being present was often enough, and shared quiet, even shared lament, does help with wellbeing. It was when taking funerals that I also saw the value of the Psalms, of ancient words that give voice to unspeakable pain.

To have a space where we allow others to express sadness is a gift. I spent time with a friend today in a writing break. She was going through a terrible time and poured it all out. At the end I said how sorry I was that this was happening for her and she thanked me for not trying to fix it, saying she would not feel able to tell me if she thought it would weigh me down. It isn't that I am not compassionate and that I don't want this hard time for my friend to end. It is that I have learned that God is closer to me in the hard times, so I will assume, as he has no favourites,[3] that he will do the same for her. I can feel free to hand her over and only do something about what she has told me if she asks me to.

If we could create spaces for people to lament and let that sit alongside praise, we would find fewer people leaving church and community when loss happens. We would find room for people to be able to stay in community even when the song of their lives is in a minor key.

The place of lament is vital in our churches and communities.

 Take Notice

The following lament was written as I took notice during the early lockdown days of the COVID-19 global pandemic. I share this here as an example of a poem or psalm I have written that was important for me to express sadness. It is a lament. I encourage you to write your own.

'Blessed are those who mourn, for they shall be comforted' (Jesus, Matt. 5:4)

'The Lord cares deeply
when his loved ones die.'[4]

You see
You weep
You are close by

But Lord
I do not get it
Why?
If you are God
Of all that's good and right
Why can't you blow away
this dark, dark night?

I cry to you
(There's no one else to cry to)
And then I hear
The whispered cheer . . .

'Blessed are the mourners'
All who weep
Blessed are those
Whose grief is deep
Blessed, honoured
Held in heaven's high esteem
Those who've lost their
Loved ones, hopes and dreams

I see the bottle of collected tears
Your nail-pierced hands
That held us through the years
Now gather every drop
Each grief-filled sign
And mingling the human and divine

You hold your wounded planet
Close to your loving heart

And weep with us

Then in the pain you start
To pour
Your comfort
And your love

No glib response
No false hope cheer
Just gentle whisper
'Child, come here'

Blessed are the mourners
Those who weep and cry
His comfort holds you
Till the day you die
And then beyond
Oh Glory, there is more
We'll one day step
Hope-filled
Tear-free
Through heaven's open door

Yet now we mourn
We need to cry
He sees, he weeps
He is close by[5]

Ruth Rice, March 2020

Give

QUESTIONS

How do you express and deal with loss and grief at the moment?

How does community help or hinder this?

What practices help you to be honest about negative emotion?

Do you have a favourite lament or song or psalm that has helped you in a difficult time?

PRAYER

Lord, take my honest words and sighs
For here I stand before your eyes
Undone
How long, O Lord, how long?
When will these minor notes give way to major song?

Resources

There are some great chapters written about trauma and lament, lament as truth-telling and corporate lament among other helpful things in *The Bible and Mental Health*, edited by Christopher Cook and Isabelle Hamley.[6]

Check out the excellent lament songs of Tim Judson on Amazon, Apple Music and Spotify.

M is for Meditation

 **Connect**

meditating . . . day and night. (Psalm 1:2, NLT)

Some Christians struggle with the idea of meditation, thinking it to be an Eastern mystical practice. I personally have this word at the top of my wellbeing lexicon. Christian meditation is God's idea, I think. If you read books about meditation or look it up online, you could be forgiven for thinking it's a weird practice for the few who are deeply spiritual. I would like to recapture it as many have done before me. Meditation is a simple way of entering fully into the presence of God. There is something very ordinary about meditation that feels almost like a waste of time. We are conditioned to be always doing and if not doing, then always thinking about things. In meditation we take a few words and repeat them over and over to bring us to a settled, still state where body, mind and soul are fully present to God. It is not mind-emptying, although there is a requirement to empty out all the clutter as you start. For me, it is mind-filling. I know many practitioners of meditation would probably find what I describe in this chapter as not pure meditation. I don't take one single word for a mantra, but choose instead a phrase each week from a psalm.

I want to persuade those who are still wondering if I'm wandering too far from Christian theology that meditation is God's idea. For me, Psalm 1 is a mandate for meditation. As the psalmist tells us, he meditates 'day and night' on 'the law of the LORD' – he uses the word '*hagah*' in Hebrew, which means to mutter, ponder, utter sounds. There is a sense of someone murmuring under their breath the same words over and over. But he meditates on something, on 'the law of the LORD'. This is not a practice that encourages you to think of nothing, to make the mind a vacant space. This is a choice to go over and over the truth, the Word of God. Not to study it or to write a sermon on it, but to murmur it. To repeat it until it settles deep within you. This is what I understand of Christian meditation. To take the Word of God and chew on it, taste it, ruminate on it: to breathe it in and out.

I believe Jesus practises this. On the cross he says very few things, but as Pete Greig points out in the excellent Prayer Course II[1] based on *God on Mute*,[2] the sayings of Jesus echo the beginning and end of Psalm 22. We can maybe surmise Jesus is meditating, murmuring his way through that psalm that he would have known and loved to take him through the worst time ever and to remind him of who he is.

In Paul's letter to the Ephesians, I spot lots of references to meditation. In Ephesians 3:18–19 Paul prays that those reading:

> may have power, together with all the Lord's holy people, to grasp how wide and long and high and deep is the love of Christ, and to know this love that surpasses knowledge – that you may be filled to the measure of all the fullness of God.[3]

Here is a description of what can happen as we meditate. As we take his Word into us and chew it over, we 'grasp' it. We don't just hear it and even understand it . . . we 'grasp' it. Then as we stay in the place of meditation, we go from grasping to knowing something that 'surpasses knowledge', which seems like a contradiction, but there is a deeper knowing than just having knowledge of something. When it settles in us as a truth, we then become filled with him.

In Ephesians 1:18 Paul prays that 'the eyes of your hearts [will be] enlightened'. Here there is a beautiful metaphor for what happens when we meditate. The heart has eyes and we see with soul vision.

When I meditate I can sometimes begin to grasp, to see with 'heart eyes', how much I am loved, how great God is: just sometimes I can see things in perspective.

> When I meditate I can sometimes begin to grasp, to see with 'heart eyes', how much I am loved.

The reason I choose to meditate on Scripture is that I believe it is powerful and not just words – it is words from God's mouth that have promised to effect change where they land. It is for this reason I prefer to take a phrase from the Bible, not just a mantra I have made up. Every person needs to unpack this practice for themselves. Here is how I do it.

 Learn

Learning to really meditate, not just write a sermon in my head

Meditation is one of those things you have to learn by doing, not just reading about or studying. I realize I find it much easier to take a phrase from God's Word and write a sermon on it, study it, or talk about it rather than meditate on it. To meditate is very different and takes practice.

So this practice came out of a time when I was feeling so unwell that I couldn't hold more than a few words in my head at a time. I was getting easily overwhelmed and confused. So I decided to read a psalm a week and then ask God to highlight just one phrase that if I went over and over it in my head, it would calm me.

Since that day in 2009 when this habit started, it has been a lifeline to me. Interestingly, today as I write I am having a low day. So instead of sitting with my cup and meditating on my psalm, I stay in bed a bit longer and begin to feel sorry for myself.

It takes me six hours of distraction before I finally take my cup and begin to breathe in and out, 'The LORD is righteous' from Psalm 11. As I do so my shoulders drop. I begin to feel the chair supporting me. I place my feet firmly on the floor and know I am set here by God. I steady my breathing. On the in breath 'The LORD is' on the out breath 'righteous'. Again. I begin to calm. The inner voices of criticism and irritation and self-pity subside. I replace my own need with the truth of God's righteous presence for a while, and even though I still feel sad, I feel less empty. His love begins to settle me. It is not deep or life-changing. It is very ordinary. But as I sit, eyes closed, breathing deeply, taking in the truth for this day, the other thoughts in my head have to displace themselves and or-bit around the truth from God's Word. If he is righteous, com-pletely good, completely kind, completely just and fair, then he knows what to do for that family member I am worrying about and that team member who is struggling. If he is righteous and he promises to clothe me in his righteousness too, then I can let go of these sinful self-pitying thoughts and be embraced in his goodness. I can breathe out my fears and breathe in his love.

This practice of sitting still with my empty cup several times a day but at the very least, for my first cuppa each day, is the basic practice of wellbeing from which this whole way of life that I am so passionate about has come.

The practice of biblical meditation is something that needs actually practising every day. It doesn't need a lot of kit and fuss. But for such a simple habit, it is so hard to actually do it. I have to set a timer on my phone so I don't kid myself I have sat for ages when it can be just a few seconds and I am itching to get on with something 'more useful', as my head keeps telling me. To actually sit still for even a few minutes, and then build that up to five minutes or so at a time is really hard and requires me to keep bringing my mind back to the phrase. Without the phrase to meditate on, for me it is impossible. My mind fills with every worrying thought and distracting images. But as I choose to really bring my whole being to the few words of the day, something wonderful can happen. The presence of God seeps into my soul again. He was always there. It was me that stopped realizing this.

 Get Active

Using this practice in community may seem a little odd. As we get active with this word 'meditation', I am suggesting that it is a helpful practice or habit to do in community. There is something very powerful about a shared silence in which all are tapping in to the presence of God by meditating on the same truth. If you have ever seen a single wind turbine reaching up into the air, you will know that it holds no power in itself but when the wind blows, the wind turbine takes that power and transfers it into energy. I always feel when I see one that this is an image of what it feels like to practice meditation. God's presence is all around like the air, the wind. But without the turbine I can fail to tap into that source of life. As I pray or meditate in this way, I grasp that presence and bring him into my daily life.

So with this image in mind, now picture a wind farm. This is a community in meditation for me. When we have sat down with the same words and enjoyed the silence together (which takes a bit of getting used to), the silence feels less scary in company.

Our 'Cup' groups, which started in my home, would enable us to learn this new skill together. After our cuppa and chat would read the psalm of the day and pick the meditation phrase. Then we would set a timer for a few minutes and just sit quietly, giving each other permission to enjoy silence and stillness together. This is inevitably when the tummy rumbles or the phone rings but we were determined to stay still and present if possible. At the end of the time allotted, we would ask each other how that went and pray for each other briefly to be able to keep practising his presence in the week.

This is not a practice we use much in our Renew spaces as there are folk who are completely new to prayer and faith and long silence can be too much. But it is a practice I still love when I am with the team or a group of fellow Renew hosts. This means that our time together in Renew prayer spaces comes from an even deeper practice of biblical meditation that we can introduce people to if they are interested and ready.

I would dearly love to see more churches giving time in small groups to this practice. There may have been times when we have felt comfortable enough to have silence, but often this is not a silence where we are together meditating on one truth. Sometimes sung worship can lead us into this collective meditation. I love sung worship. It has been one of the saddest things about the pandemic restrictions of 2020–21 . . . not being able to sing together. It is a strong form of corporate meditation, as is spoken liturgy. But I would still say that for me, shared silent meditation on the same phrase from the Bible has an even more wonderful effect on my wellbeing. We are not all alone in our wellbeing needs, and as we come together in the act of meditation, we can feel the presence of God more powerfully in the space between us.

 Take Notice

I remember vividly being invited to the home of a wonderful young lady who was dying from advanced cancer. Her friends who were Christians had been meeting with her to pray and to share Jesus with her for some weeks.

But the session I was invited to was a really hard one. A family member of this girl was present, and extremely distressed. Our hearts were breaking for her as she expressed some of this and asked why I thought God wasn't doing anything. I had no words. No answers.

A friend who was a lifeguard had once told me that if you go to help a drowning person, take something that floats or they will pull you under. We all felt in danger of being pulled under that day. Indeed, where was God?

As the minister I was asked to say something, do something. I had nothing! So I pulled out my 'thing that floats', my practice of Bible meditation. It happened to be 'The Lord is my stronghold' that week from Psalm 27 – 'The LORD is the stronghold of my life' (v. 1). As all tearful eyes were on me, I encouraged everyone to take hold of their cup in order to know they were held. I asked everyone to sit comfortably, to feel the chair beneath them, holding them as God was holding us. And I asked them to breathe in and out the phrase 'The Lord is my stronghold'. I left it a lot more than a few minutes and although on the surface I was meditating, in my head I was panicking like crazy. What will I say when we open our eyes, Lord? I still have nothing . . . 'The Lord is my stronghold'. What would I feel like if this was me? . . . 'The Lord is my stronghold' . . . How can I make this better, what can I do? . . . 'The Lord is my stronghold'. The room was still and peaceful, but I knew I would need to stop this at some point and face the pain.

As we opened our eyes, I was amazed. There were tears rolling down people's faces and the relative of the young lady who was so poorly came across the room and embraced me. 'The Lord is my stronghold,' she whispered. Something had happened. Some mysterious divine exchange that I will never understand to this day. God can speak for himself! Who knew? No words from me were needed. His stronghold was holding us. I was not the saviour. The moment of meditation had held within it all of the power and presence of God that this woman needed for that moment.

I was floored and humbled. How could we make this more available and accessible to all? That is what the Renew spaces have been all about, to be honest. The hope that many more broken and hurting people will learn to meet with God in this way. So that when we have no words, we don't try to make some up and make things worse; we let him speak.

> When we have no words, we don't try to make some up and make things worse; we let God speak.

Give

QUESTIONS

Have you tried meditation? What was good and not so good about it?

What do you feel about Bible mediation versus other mantra meditation?

Do you think it is possible to meditate with others? Have you tried it?

What would help you to start this practice?

What do you think about singing as a form of meditation?

PRAYER

Lord, lead me deeper into you
Bring me to that point where
All I need is your presence
All I want is your peace
All I can see is your face

Resources

The series of talks in the eBook by John Main (ed. Laurence Freeman), *Fully Alive: An Introduction to Christian Meditation.*

N is for Names

Connect

I have called you by name . . . (Isaiah 43:1)

'Names not labels' is one of the values that has become a slogan of Renew Wellbeing. This came from talking to the lady who told us that she loved coming to renew37 as now 'someone knows my name'. This still upsets me to my core to think people can go all week and not hear their names mentioned. Our names are the first thing given to us, whether we like them or not. I can remember wishing my parents had called me Aimee. Not just Amy but Aimee, meaning 'loved' in French. I always felt 'Ruth' was the sort of name attached to an elderly aunt with facial hair. I do actually fit that descriptor now, although my lovely nieces would be too kind to point that out.

But today I'm glad of this name. I appreciate the value and thought attached to it. In the Bible, names were vital. They were full of meaning and often designed to be prophetic. Names seem to be very important to the writers of the Bible. Often names are listed for no apparent reason and I have skipped through whole chapters of Numbers wondering why it was necessary to include so much detail. There are thirty-five names mentioned in less than ten verses in Numbers 1.[1] In fact,

I used to wonder if they were just there to make it harder for the person doing the public reading of the Bible on a Sunday.

But these detailed genealogies have also been a source of fascination to me. This big, sweeping story of God's dealings with humans is with one after another. Individuals obviously matter a lot, and so do their names. The Bible talks of God knowing our name.[2] It speaks of our names being 'engraved' on his hands (Isa. 49:16) and in John 10:3, Jesus speaks of us as sheep being known 'by name' by the good shepherd. He knows my name, he calls me by name. I am precious to him and so is my name.

In the Hebrew the word 'name' is *shem* and forms part of the word that means breath. There is an indication that a name is the very life and character of a person.

Not least with God himself. The name of God could not even be spoken, it was thought to be so holy. Yahweh is two Hebrew sounds, literally meaning 'I am who I am'.[3] I love the fact that to say this in Hebrew is like inhaling and exhaling; there is breath in the very word. God's name is so vital, so important. There are much better scholars than me who will be able to help you study the importance of the name of God. Identity is tied up in name and in God's name so much is communicated, so much power and love is held within this unchanging name.

What I want to convey in my simple way is that for wellbeing, not only do I need to be known by name, but also I need to know the name of the One who holds me. My identity is not just tied up in knowing the name my parents gave me, but in being held and found under the name of the One who calls himself 'I AM'.[4] This is a name that will never change, go out of fashion, or be altered in its identity in any way. This name is the name to beat all other names and this is the name I place my name within. My wellbeing, our wellbeing is kept most safe in this name.

My wellbeing, our wellbeing is kept most safe in this name.

 Learn

Name-calling, but in a good way!

One of my habits for wellbeing is to start each day once I have meditated by speaking out the name of God in morning prayers. Psalm 103:1 calls us to: 'Bless the LORD, O my soul, and all that is within me, bless his holy name!' So I then begin to thank him for who he is:

Prince of Peace
Creator and sustainer of all things
Emmanuel
Wonderful
Counsellor . . .[5]

The list goes on.

As I begin to recall his name, I settle my restless mind and heart. He is still the same each day. I am safe in him. I am secure. My identity is in this name. As I do this I am speaking to my own soul and asking, 'Ruth, what is in your mind and heart today?' ('all that is within me'[6]). As I try to answer myself honestly, using my journal if that helps, I try to speak kindly to myself.

A number of years ago at some training event, I was asked to send myself a letter. It was to be written to my younger self with some advice. The event organizer then sent us the letters when we had forgotten all about them. I was so shocked to see my own handwriting and was even more shocked as I ripped open the letter and read the contents that I had forgotten about and had written in something of a hurry. If I had received that letter from anyone else I would have been upset by it. It was rude, bullying and critical. I berated myself for almost everything. I would never have written any of those things to another living human being. And I started the letter 'Dear Ruth'. There was nothing 'dear' in it. No love or self-compassion. Just self-criticism and ill-disguised self-loathing.

It was an eye-opener and I repented. I asked God to help me love this Ruth person. To see her as he did. Every now and then, I get a glimpse of God's love for this Ruth. He is delighted in her, in me, and I feel humbled all over again.

I am trying to speak to myself these days with the same kindness I would a friend. I don't always manage it. I spent so many years making jokes at my own expense. It's a hard habit to break.

Learning to see my name held within his name means that on the days when I cannot see a single good thing about my identity, I can know that God has chosen me and loves me just for who I am.

 **Get Active**

'Names not labels' is one of the big values for all our Renew spaces. When someone enters the space, we don't take down

details of diagnoses etc., we just ask for a name. To be known by name is enough. I will never forget the lady telling me she loved Renew as it was the only place where people knew her name. How sad. How awful that so many people are going un-named in our communities.

> To be known by name is enough.

At our Renew spaces, the person welcoming at the door will show folk around and simply ask for a name, and will introduce people by name, not by position in the organization. By so doing no one really knows who is a host and who is a regular.

Many of those visiting have said how refreshing this is when so many of their interactions with services require them to give so much more detail. To be simply known by their name in that place at that time releases everyone from having to have any other word attached to them to get attention.

Our local churches are at the heart of the Renew movement because for centuries the church has been forming communities based solely on acceptance of each other by name. I know this has become overcomplicated over the years, but communities of Jesus-following disciples have always been called by name by him.

The local church is one community it should be possible to belong to regardless of any other label attached to you. A name is enough.

The Renew centre attached to the local church gives more time to explore what is behind each person's name so that their name can be remembered and used. To have your name spoken and remembered is a basic human need. To have it used with love and acceptance is what God is committed to.

 **Take Notice**

Mac had been called many names. His antisocial habits hadn't helped. He knew that. But he had sunk so low over the years of difficult relationships and disappointments that the bottle seemed to hold more answers that his friends or family.

It wasn't that others didn't try to love him, try to reach out to him, but the labels stuck like glue to him. The addictions came with tape attached and he felt no one could see him, Mac, any more. It wasn't anyone else's fault and he didn't blame people for wanting to get the labels sorted. Lots of people had tried to unstick them over the years. He just kept sticking them right back over the cracks to protect himself.

Every clinic, every group, every appointment and hostel all used his name, of course, but he was aware that they only knew his name because of his label.

When he walked into the little Renew space that he had been told about, he braced himself to give a life history so that he could sign up for this nice, warm bit of help. He was surprised when there was no paperwork to fill in, just a friendly face asking his name.

'Mac,' he said. 'My name is Mac.'

'And what do you like to do, Mac?' came the reply.

Like to do? He wasn't ready for this question. He was ready to assure them he hadn't had a drink that day and that he was ready to accept the few sessions they could offer.

'Oh, I like photography!' he said.

Mac reached in his coat pocket and took out the last few photos he had taken and printed out. He was proud of them. He found himself sitting at a big kitchen table clutching a cuppa and showing them to those who gathered round, full of admiration for his work.

He imagined these other folk must have troubles, too, like him, but no one seemed to be asking about what was wrong with him, just marvelling at what was right with him. It felt good to be Mac the photographer again.

He promised to come back the next day and bring more shots he had taken, so they could frame them for the walls of this lovely community space.

The next day and next, no one asked for his life history but everyone knew his name. He began to trust these kind people with his story and was amazed when they still welcomed him, still didn't try to fix him.

Here he had found a home, a place he was known by name not label. Maybe it was time to let the label go too.

Give

QUESTIONS

Do you like your name? Are you named after someone?

What is your favourite name, and why?

What labels have you found helpful and unhelpful in your life?

PRAYER

(In response to one of our regulars at renew37 telling us that she could go all week without hearing her name mentioned.)

My name inscribed on eternal palms
My days

Written and planned held in stronger arms
Our name
His church
Sweet bride, chosen one
His name
Our battle cry
And soul song
This name
Above all other names
In whom our name belongs
For unnamed unknown unloved ones
Who spend a day
A week, a year
Not hearing
They are loved
And often when their name is heard
The name that came
With life breath at created word
That precious name
Called out
In clinical spaces attached to notes
From officious faces
For those whose labels show before their names
Who have not heard
The whisper of the Father, Spirit
Son who came
The ones who no one knows their name
He calls you 'Bride, come out
From death-filled tomb' and breathing in his life

Breathe out
And make some room
A room
A space
Where all are known
By name and face

An excerpt from 'Now Someone Knows My Name' by Ruth Rice, March 2018[7]

Resources

John Mark Comer, *God Has a Name*. This is a great book looking closely at what God says about himself in Exodus 34 and the difference that can make to our relationship with him.

O is for One

 **Connect**

One thing have I asked of the LORD . . . (Psalm 27:4)

One. This seems like a bit of a departure. Surely one is a number, not really a word. But for my wellbeing alphabet, this has to be there. One is a very key number when it comes to my own wellbeing and the running of a good Renew space. One thing. A simple, single-minded approach. One person. Enough to make me want to do something completely different. One, a key number in the economy of heaven.

Let's look at how to connect better with God with this word, one. Some of my favourite Gospel stories involve Jesus going out of his way for one single person.

John 4 tells the story of Jesus encountering the woman at the well. It says 'he had to pass through Samaria' (v. 4) on his journey. I ask myself if he really had to. Most good Jews would have gone out of their way to go around Samaria. This was not a place you would expect a rabbi to visit. This was a place to avoid. But Jesus 'had to' go there, I believe, because he knew this woman would be at this well, lonely and rejected. She was collecting water, not at the time other women would be there for a catch-up because she was the one they would be talking about, gossiping about. She avoided them and came when the sun was at its highest and no one would be there, to avoid the awkward conversations and stares. She had not had a good set of life opportunities – some might say, choices. She had a hidden story. But Jesus waited at the well at the time of day she would be there and engaged with her.

He first asks her for a drink. This again would be unheard of. He is risking his reputation right there. But he chooses to come in vulnerability, in need, empty-handed, and ask for what she can help him with. No other man has treated her like this.

We gain so much from this attitude in our Renew spaces. Coming empty-handed, not in power, and having room to receive the gift of the other, honouring what each other carries.

Then he engages in theological debate with her and answers her questions. Most religious leaders would never engage with a woman in this way, let alone a Samaritan woman. Here Jesus treats her with respect and honour.

Then he appears to point out her faults, her darkest secret, as he asks her to fetch her husband and says what he knows of her difficult relationship history. But I don't see judgement in what Jesus says here. I see him telling her he knows what she is hiding, what she thinks makes her unlovable and causes her to be isolated. He says he knows and offers her 'living water' (v. 10). He is saying that he sees her and still accepts her. Maybe he is even saying that he knows she has been badly treated and he won't be one of the men joining in. He comes to restore, to bring hope, to bring life. She is hooked and runs to the town to invite the very people she was avoiding to 'Come, see a man' (v. 29) who she has found something different in.

That one encounter with one woman that Jesus went out of his way for would not be the way we might set up an evangelistic campaign to reach great numbers. But through this one woman, many would come to faith (v. 39). I tend to believe it was not even that strategic. I like to think Jesus felt his time was well spent just being with the one.

Then there is the encounter with Peter at the end of the Gospel of John. One of my all-time favourite characters, Peter, hot-headed and impulsive. The one who said he would die for Jesus (Matt. 26:35) has let him down badly right when Jesus needed him, denied he even knew him (Matt. 26:69–75). He is desperate and sad and even knowing Jesus is alive again is not enough to calm him. He has gone back to his fishing, something he knew how to do, and finds he can't even do that. Then having fished all night and caught nothing, Jesus brings him to fruitfulness in his natural gift before restoring him to fruitfulness in the kingdom.

The risen Christ has decided that one of the few resurrection appearances would involve him cooking breakfast on the beach for his weary friends and going out of his way to restore Peter. This is a story that makes me love Jesus all the more. I have had my fair share of self-induced weary work and have found an encounter with Jesus to be this sweet.

This breakfast-cooking Saviour! What a thing to do for his friends. And the conversation with Peter gets right to the heart of the three betrayals with three restoration words. He appoints this one who has proven his infidelity to the important task of sheep feeder for the dear folk who will believe (John 21:15–19). Peter is undone by the encounter. The love and forgiveness alone would have been amazing but the trust Jesus puts in him to restore purpose to him is stunning.

The encounter with Mary at her home, with her sister flapping around criticizing her for sitting at Jesus' feet with the disciples looking on, waiting for Jesus to lecture Mary in how to change the world by hard work, also has me floored. In Luke 10 we see the disciples on a fast-track follower programme in healing, evangelism and social action. With mission trips and stories, they are learning how to make disciples and then at the end of the chapter, when they think they have the activists' guide to Christianity all sewn up, Jesus takes them to Mary and Martha's house. Here I feel for the disciples looking on trying to make sense of this encounter.

In response to the accusation of laziness from her sister, Jesus actually reprimands the one doing all the serving. You can almost hear the disciples thinking, 'Surely he wants us to serve others? What is going on here?' He says 'Martha, Martha, you are anxious and troubled about many things, but *one* thing is necessary. Mary has chosen the good portion, which will not be taken away from her' (vv. 41,42, my italics).

 Learn

Learning to know your no as well as your yes

The call from God to plant Renew centres came through a dream as I was reading Judges 4. At the time I was involved in loads of things that I loved. I was Mum and wife, of course, and leading a lovely church full-time, but I was also taking teenagers on life-changing trips to Africa and planning a trip to visit persecuted Christians. I was spreading myself thinly over a large number of activities as if I had learned nothing at all from the breakdown that I was still recovering from. I was so happy to be able to get involved in life again that I forgot that I only had one life.

The Africa trips were so wonderful. I love travel and, even though it was time-consuming and exhausting and it wasn't every year, I was planning the next one as soon as I got back. My friend Helen who organized and ran the trips was so good at the details that I tagged along and helped make contacts with local schools and helped fundraise. I had had the privilege of taking two of my own children on such trips and had seen the life-changing effect it could have, bringing someone from a culture of privilege alongside those who had less in terms of riches but were often richer by far in terms of faith and community. The two-way learning about wellbeing in those cross-cultural settings was fascinating.

What I hadn't learned was that just because I loved something or enjoyed something, that didn't mean it was my something to do. Trying to do everything was taking me down a fast track to burnout again. God stepped in and made it very clear to me that he was opening doors. I kept reading things about doors opening, and having people pray for me and say they saw doors opening.

> Just because I loved something or enjoyed something, that didn't mean it was my something to do.

So quick was I to try a new thing that I instantly thought this meant more visits with another organization close to my heart – Open Doors.[1] I was in the process of arranging a trip to an area of the world where Christians were persecuted, to bring them support, when God stepped in again and turned the volume up some more.

This was when I was on a course based on the remarkable book called *7 Deadly Sins of Women in Leadership*,[2] run by my friends Kate Coleman and Cham Kaur Man. It was life-changing. I recommend it to any leader, not just women.

While exploring the need for personal vision, I heard the clear voice of God calling me to set up Renew centres. The detail of this is in my first book.

The call to one thing was a call to follow one Lord, but also for me, a call to have one vision, to be less distracted so I could do one thing well.

 **Get Active**

For us now at Renew Wellbeing, the central charity helping churches set up Renew spaces, this commitment to one means that we will happily help churches open centres for just one person. If one person is helped by a space, we think it is worth our time and effort. We will run a course for one or two people, drive miles to have a cuppa with one person. We have invested in more team members so that we can still have the conversations with the ones and twos and keep this personal.

It also means we have to know what our no is as well as our yes. We are asked to speak at lots of things, to get involved with lots of things, and they are all interesting and worthy. But we are learning, I am learning, to say no to things that are someone else's to do.

One thing I learned when working with the Cinnamon Network[3] team was the concept bullseye. This is a sort of dart-board bullseye drawing of concentric circles where we were encouraged to write in the centre the thing or things that we felt were absolutely key to our charities. These were the things we were passionate about and that God had called us to. I wrote: 'Be prayerful, be present, and be in partnership.' Then in the next circle we had to write what things might be important in setting up a centre, but not essential. I wrote things like 'A nice café-style space', 'A team of at least four people', etc. Then as the circles went out, the things became less and less vital. In the outer circle we were encouraged to write what was important but maybe not ours to do. I wrote 'Change the entire culture of church' and 'Help churches do other pioneering things that are not Renew spaces'. This was what I really wanted to see happen but my call was simple and clear. I refer back to that concept bullseye often. I wonder what yours would look like.

It means no more Africa trips for me at the moment. It means me choosing the simple task of speaking about my broken story and how to set up a Renew space over and over again, when there are times I would like to try loads of new things. It means this book is very simple.

 ## Take Notice

On one of my trips to Africa I saw this single-minded commitment in beautiful technicolour. I visited a project in Ethiopia run by Ellilta International.[4] The organization has been helping women to get free from prostitution and into employment for more than twenty years. Run by locals for locals, these people have been offering the same simple programme to twenty women a year, chosen because they were really committed to the idea and wanted to be free.

I was so impressed by the focus on what really amounted to a few women. The temptation to spread a little help very widely was all too evident when we visited. The need was intense.

Many women had moved to the city on the promise of jobs that didn't exist and had been effectively sold into slavery on the streets. Girls as young as 10. It was heart-breaking to see girls standing in rows on the dark streets.

How these people could choose who to help was beyond me. But they selected carefully and prayerfully. They matched the woman's income for a year and got their children into education. They found training for the woman, and the success rate in terms of staying off the street was around 90 per cent.

The focus on the one was working, and since starting in 1996, Ellilta International have helped more than 1,000 women escape prostitution.

I was in awe of this consistent, simple, focused work. I still am.

It did mean that many of the other desperate needs in that city were left to other organizations to help with. To be focused on doing one thing well, this charity had to know what to say no to as well as what to say yes to. The greater the needs around you, the harder this is to do. So many churches and organizations spread themselves so thinly that they wear themselves out, and in letting folk down they give the impression that God has let people down. There is too much at stake for us to over-offer. Let's learn to do one thing well.

> There is too much at stake for us to over-offer. Let's learn to do one thing well.

Give

QUESTIONS

Can you articulate what your one thing is in terms of your inner life with God and your calling or purpose? Not everyone can, so please don't worry if you can't.

Is there a time when you feel God has singled you out in some way?

Would you be prepared to keep showing up in a Renew space if only one person ever came?

PRAYER

Matthew 13:44–46
Seek *one thing*

One treasure
One pearl
One thing
I seek your kingdom
Your presence
Each day this week

One heart
For one goal
One joy
One prize
To see
All things
With your eyes

It's simple it's costly
Not easy
It's true
But to give in simplicity
I give my *all*
To you

All thoughts and
All dreams
All plans
And all fears
I give you my minutes
My hours

Days and
Years

I give you my treasure
I give you my dross
I give you my moments
Of success and
Of loss

I give you my heart
I give all to gain you
Your kingdom, your reign
Give the old for the new

But the pearl I have found
And the treasure I win
Is true love and forgiveness
And freedom from sin

The things I held tightly
Were heavy to me
Now you hold them
I hold life
Divine swap
I'm free

Resources

Check out: Ellilta International in Ethiopia: http://www.ellilta.org/what-we-do

Open Doors: https://www.opendoorsuk.org/

Kate Coleman, *7 Deadly Sins of Women in Leadership.*

$\boxed{\text{P}}$ is for Present

 **Connect**

Draw near to God, and he will draw near to you. (James 4:8)

This was such a difficult letter for me. I have so many wellbeing words that start with p. Peace, partnership, prayer, pause, presence, people, places, psalms. Our three principles start with P. Presence, partnership and prayer. My five points for pioneers wanting to engage in mission start with p. So, how do I choose? I really want to choose 'prayer' as there is no wellbeing without prayer, but I feel that runs through everything I have written already, so I choose the word 'presence'. For my own wellbeing this has been such a key word to get my head round. Present. Here and now. In this moment. I spent such a lot of time in my head either in the past that I could do nothing about, or worrying about a future that was not yet here. Learning to be in the present has been so healing for me.

> Learning to be in the present has been so healing for me.

So first, let's connect with God's perspective on the word 'present' or 'presence'. To be present is about presence, so please bear with me if I swap and change between the two words.

In the Hebrew the word we translate as presence is '*panim*' or '*panah*'. *Panim* means face and *panah* means to turn around. Hebrew is, of course, more complex and rich than this, but these two meanings brought together help me grasp a little more of what presence looks like. For God to be present involves his face and him turning to us.

I spent many years teaching small children. If a child was distressed or misbehaving, the first thing I would do was get down to that child's level and ask them to look at me. Once we had eye contact, it became easier to work out what was going on and to bring some comfort or discipline, depending on the situation. I remember being completely at a loss when in one class of 5-year-olds. I taught two lovely boys with autistic tendencies who both refused any sort of eye contact, especially with each other. And the conflicts were often with one another. One memorable circle time when the children loved to do the good old 'show and tell', I can still see both boys refusing to face each other while they talked about their precious item. Both boys faced outwards in the circle until the other had finished talking. In so doing they were quite content, but it did make for a tricky time at the end of an even trickier day. Eventually I made each boy their own little shelters or dens which they could go to whenever needed and even talk from during circle time if they wished. Once the pressure for eye contact had gone, they even happily shared news and toys with each other from their safe dens.

How often I find myself in my relationship with God behaving just like these boys. I am there but I am not present. God is present to us at all times. His name means presence. He is the great 'I am'. From the very beginning of the Bible we see his presence, and in Exodus 33:14 he promises outright to be present with his people. Moses, it says, talks to him 'face to face' – this is the word *panim* – 'as a man speaks to his friend' (Exod. 33:11).

Jesus comes to bring all of us the opportunity for this sort of presence with God. 1 Corinthians 13:12 talks about us only seeing 'in part' now but one day seeing 'face to face'; the Greek *prosopon*, having a similar sense of the Hebrew *panim*. So by the New Testament it is not just the great and the good, the Moses characters, who get to experience and know his presence – because of the cross and resurrection of Jesus, it is for all of us. James 4:8 says, 'Draw near to God, and he will draw near to you.'

The presence of God is the secret to wellbeing for me. Which is good news, as he is always present. So the task for me is to find ways to turn my face to his face.

 Learn

Showing up: Where's your head at?

Learning to be present to God, myself and others is probably the most difficult practice of all the letters in the alphabet so far. Even as I sit down to write this chapter, I first turn my chair to face the window. I get a cuppa, then get the dog settled at my feet. OK, that is preparation. I gaze around at the garden, remembering yesterday's pottering. This could still be classed as meditation. I do my actual meditation and write in my journal. I get the laptop ready and write notes in my big A–Z notebook. Then I spot there's a gap in the garden that could do with a bench. Now I'm distracted. Next I find myself spending twenty minutes googling garden benches and it is not before I head to the dreaded online giant purchasing page that I catch myself not being present; until this point it all felt very justified. I then have to choose to be truly present to this laptop, this letter, this thought to you, my readers. I need to be present to my own heart as I try to dig deeper into wellbeing.

I am penning these lines at a difficult time in our shared history. Lockdown for COVID-19 is beginning to ease, but it feels like a long time until I get to see my family, hug my kids, visit my friends, swim in the sea. And all these things, happening sometime in the future, feel like essentials for my wellbeing since they have been removed. But as I write I realize all I truly need is in this present moment, right here with the God who holds me. I am not saying that the loss of other things doesn't make me sad, it does, and I acknowledge and accept that sadness as part of how much I love the things I cannot have. But if I can bring my anxious thoughts and settle in this moment, there is still wholeness and wellbeing to be had, even without the things I think I really need.

My habits around being truly present to God and myself are many and varied and constitute the bulk of my whole day's challenge. There is that fine balance between planning ahead, reflecting on the past and dwelling in the present moment. I have been increasingly aware during a year stuck at home of how much my thought-life lives primarily in the future or the past. As a human being, a mum, wife, friend and the leader of a charity, there is a need to reflect well on past triumphs and failures so I learn from them. There is also a need to plan well for the future when you lead a team, have a family, or want to live healthily in your own skin. However, I am aware that instead of visiting the future to plan and the past to learn, I can dwell there. I can be far too present in times that are not present.

I am keen not just to write words that sound true but to ground them in what that looks like for me. So, even as I write this, I am thinking about the other things I want to do today. They lurk somewhere at the back of my mind and I need to keep putting them back there or they make me less present to this writing. I find myself wondering how long it might take me to complete the chapter so that I can do the next thing rather than truly settling my heart, my head and my whole self to this task in hand with true presence. This is what God is present in. He is right here with me. So when I disappear off to the next thing in my head, I feel less present with God and more anxious about what needs doing that I am not doing because I am doing this!

I remember being really inspired by reading about both Brother Lawrence, a seventeenth-century monk who became fascinated and captivated by God's presence, and also Frank Laubach, a twentieth-century missionary to the Philippines who decided to make his whole life an experiment of being present.[1]

Brother Lawrence challenged me to truly be present in even the most menial of tasks. He tried to live as if there were only him and God in the whole world, and his relationship with God was all that mattered. This may seem a bit escapist and I am fairly sure the monastic life of the seventeenth century would not have suited me. But there is so much that draws my heart about the way this determination made Brother Lawrence do everything he did with his whole mind and heart. He found God to be as present to him in the busy kitchen as in the quiet prayer times. He made no distinction between secular and sacred and therefore lived fully in the moment in which he believed God to be truly present. When I am rushing grumpily through doing the dishes so I can get into something more important, I think of Brother Lawrence. When I am resenting the time I am taking to clean the house as I want to do something more holy or more fun, I think of Brother Lawrence.

Frank Laubach fascinates me as he tried to follow Brother Lawrence's example in a twentieth-century world where he was not cloistered away in a monastery. He put a few actual habits around the challenge, which I always find more helpful than thinking there are some very holy people who can manage this sort of presence and that the rest of us are doomed to struggle with a distracted life.

Having said that, Frank Laubach does go further than I feel able to. He writes on 23 March 1930:

> Can I bring the Lord back to my mind-flow every few seconds so that God shall always be in my mind? I choose to make the rest of my life an experiment in answering this question.[2]

The thing that captivated me here was not just the idea of being always present to God, but the whole idea of making your life an experiment in something. I decided then and there to make my life an experiment in the practice of wellbeing, of the wellbeing found by being truly present to God, myself and others. What comforted me was the idea that even if I failed miserably, this was part of the experiment. I was not setting myself up to try too hard to be something I am not, but to be single-minded in the way I approached my own inner and outer habits of being present. To learn from what I tried.

For each of us, these habits will be different. My simple practices with the cup, the Psalms, the prayers, the hobbies and certain spaces all help me to make my life a practice of being truly present to the God who I believe is already ever-present.

 Get Active

This sense of presence is found most often in nature for me. To walk by water, to sit and look at a tree, to plunge into a water-fall, or swim in the sea. These things all bring me into a state of being truly present to the moment in which I live and breathe with God and others.

This presence is found not only when we take time out on our own, but I find so much of the presence of God in being present to others. There is so much in the Bible about community that it would be impossible to read it and think a life isolated from others was healthy. I need other people, even though I am determined to find my all in God. I see who God is more fully when I see him in others.

The gift we bring to another of our presence is a gift that shows them love – God's love. In our Renew spaces the only thing we bring is our presence. So often I find myself wondering how these spaces work. What is it that makes them feel so special and have such a sense of wellbeing in them? I am spotting that it is a commitment to host God's presence in our prayer spaces and a commitment to be present to each other, not run around trying to serve and fix each other.

> The gift we bring to another of our presence is a gift that shows them love – God's love.

181

This is so hard for a recovering evangelistic activist. Even when we had our first Renew space I had to be reminded to sit down and join in. The need I have in me to get my worth and value from what others think of me, or how I can help them, is extreme. The antidote for me is to sit equally at a table and join in a simple hobby or activity. Being present in this way to my own needs as well as to the gift of the other means that the power dynamic, the them and us, is dismantled and true well-being can flow between us.

I know that it is absolutely possible to be truly present in a helping capacity too; good counsellors, companions, carers all know this. But for me the temptation is to step beyond my skill set and try to give more than I receive, so that I feel better about myself. In sitting together at a table and finding a common interest and listening to each other, I have found out so much about myself too. This sort of presence needs lots of practice. It is not often found. We prefer lanyards and roles with labels and counters between us to protect us from the reality of each other's present world.

 **Take Notice**

Bob knew a lot about being present. He lived alone and had done for some time. He lived outdoors, mostly, and worked with the rhythms of nature. He was present to each season and to the soil and the sun. He acknowledged a higher power but wouldn't call it God. Bob's trouble was that he was also truly present only to himself.

He was lonely.

He would wake each day and greet the birds and animals around him. He knew how to engage with the world in a healthy way. He had worked out the hard way how to protect his heart from others who would be toxic for him. He stopped and chatted to those he saw on his walks.

But he was lonely.

He tended well to his wellbeing as far as he was able by himself, and often felt a sense of peace and tranquillity that he knew had been missing when he lived too close to other people.

But he was lonely

Bob had many hobbies that brought him joy. He knew lots about the good earth and growing. He loved music and art and wrote books about other worlds. His wellbeing habits had been honed over time and through many trials.

But Bob was lonely.

One day, as he walked the streets, he came across a café that looked a bit different to the ones round the town where he felt too different to even go in; where he felt that if he did go in, he would feel more lonely because of the happy groups of friends into which he would not be welcomed.

But this café seemed to be serving nothing and inviting everyone to bring and share. He popped home and picked up some home-grown produce and some art he was working on and tentatively put his head round the door.

It was only when he entered the room that he realized what day it was. They often all felt the same to him. It was Christmas Eve and he hadn't even remembered. The lady who welcomed him invited him to join the game they were playing and grabbed a hot chocolate for him. He placed his contribution in the middle of the table and after introductions, the game continued. Some folk wandered over to the café next door and came back with mince pies, some sat on the sofa and leafed through a newspaper. It seemed OK to just be here. No one seemed to be trying to get him to open up or get help. He felt accepted and, as the session drew to a close, the lady told him they would be closed for a few days but then were open every weekday and he was welcome to pop in whenever and join in whatever was happening; he realized he was not lonely that day.

As he left he said quietly to the lady who was tidying away the game, 'Thank you, you don't know what a luxury it is to have someone present with you on a day like today.'

To his surprise, the woman's face crumpled and tears leaked from her eyes.

'It was nothing,' she said. 'We were playing the game at home anyway. And you're right, I didn't know about the luxury of presence. But I want to learn. See you next week?'

With that, Bob headed home with a spring in his step, planning which of his many wellbeing activities would translate well to the little café so he could help people with their wellbeing next week.

Ah, the luxury of presence.

Give

QUESTIONS

What do you find hardest about being present?

Which activities help you be truly in the moment?

Could you imagine being present to others, even people you don't know, in the way described above?

PRAYER

This moment
This breath
This day
This task
Lord, help me to be truly here, I ask
The present

Of this minute
As a gift I now receive
And opening it carefully
Choosing to dwell prayerfully
Your presence is in the present
And being truly present to you
I will believe.

Resources

Brother Lawrence and Frank Laubach, *Practising His Presence*.

Q is for Quiet

 **Connect**

Be still, and know that I am God. (Psalm 46:10)

The idea of me and quiet for those who know me is laughable. I am one of those people, or used to be one of those people, who get slightly panicked by gaps in conversation and feel the need to fill them with inane platitudes. I was the kind of person who sensed a quiet moment coming from 100 paces and headed it off at the pass with a joke or a conversation deflection if it all got too pensive and quiet in a room. I learned the hard way to be quiet. I am not saying this was God's doing; I did it to myself without his help. I literally wore my voice out. My breakdown began with voice loss after periods of laryngitis that I ignored and carried on through. When warned by the doctor to rest my voice, I whispered as loudly as many people can speak and just carried on. I couldn't sing, but that was maybe a mercy for others. So I know about quiet being vital. I often wonder, if I had understood the value of quiet years ago, if I had been taught how to be comfortable with silences and embrace them as a life lesson at school, then I may not have overused my voice box for years and worn it out. Who knows?

The idea of quiet was and is God's idea, I think. Before creation we are told the Spirit of God was 'hovering over the face of the waters' (Gen. 1:2), and as you read this there is a sense of deep quietness. Into this, God breathes all sorts of life, including our good selves, and he chose to give us voices and the ability to make a lot of noise. So I don't believe quiet and silence is of more value to God than sound, but I do think he meant there to be both. Throughout the creation story there is rest and activity, evening and morning, sounds and quiet.

> I don't believe quiet and silence is of more value to God than sound, but I do think he meant there to be both.

When God shows up to restore the weary prophet Elijah, he appears to him not in a mighty, noisy wind, or an earthquake, but in a 'low whisper' (1 Kgs 19:11–13).

When Jesus wanted to pray he took himself off to quiet places (Luke 5:16).

When Isaiah prophesies so powerfully about God's presence with his people, he says 'in quietness and in trust shall be your strength' (Isa. 30:15). The Hebrew word used here for quietness is *shaqat*, also meaning idleness and rest. There is a sense of quietness feeling like a waste of people's ability to do things, to make noise, to be busy. Quietness in this verse is equated to rest, which we know to be important for our wellbeing. But so often rest can be translated as a time full of TV, music, or other people's company. In short, we don't allow ourselves much quiet time.

One of the most beautiful verses in the Bible includes God making us quiet. In Zephaniah 3:17 God promises to 'rejoice over [us] with singing' (NIV) and to 'quiet [us] by his love'. The Hebrew word here is *charash* meaning silent, also meaning to engrave, cut into something. It is deep and hints at a change being made in the moment of silence. Isn't it fascinating that we take this and reverse it so often? We sing over God and rejoice and make lots of noise and call it worship. And God does tell us to do that too, so please understand me. I am all for singing and making a 'joyful noise to the LORD' (Ps. 100:1). But the engraving of God's heart on ours happens when he quiets us 'by his love'. I have the image of a baby being shushed to sleep in a parent's arms here. There is a deep peacefulness that is a rare feeling in our everyday lives full of noise and activity.

Before we come to look at why we need to be quiet, we must address the times when it feels like God is quiet; indeed, when God is silent. In his book *God on Mute*[1] Pete Greig explores the pain in his own life when dealing with unanswered prayer. Psalms 13, 28 and 44, to name but a few places in the Bible, tell of times when God seems to have vanished. I know in my own life, during that difficult year I was not hearing from God all the time, or enjoying a deep peace of spending time with him alone. No, most of the time there seemed to be an aching void where I expected God to be.

Many have spoken of this seeming absence of a God who we know to be ever-present. How can this be? It is a mystery. There can be reasons for his silence that lie in our own sin. But very often there are no reasons we can think of at all, and we are left wondering if God's silence means he has left us or he just doesn't care enough to answer. This is the reality Jesus must have felt in the wilderness and on the cross. His cry as the sin of the world separated him from the Father, 'My God, my God, why have you forsaken me?' (Matt. 27:46) is an echo of Psalm 22:1. In his death, Jesus identifies with our own sense of despair at a seemingly silent God. I suppose when I look at the state of my own fickle heart I am increasingly amazed, not at God's sometimes seeming absence, but at the fact that I ever feel his presence and hear his voice. It is so undeserved that a mere mortal full of self and sin should be able to commune with a pure, holy God. That is the miracle of the cross. The quietness of God makes the voice of God all the sweeter to me.

That whisper when I was unwell assuring me of his love, 'Ruth, I couldn't love you any more than I do right now and I will never love you any less' was so beautiful, so unexpected, because it came out of the complete silence of not having heard God for months.

A musician will tell you the beauty of a piece of music can lie in the spaces, the silences between the notes.

Some of the Psalms were written with the word 'Selah' at intervals within them. In fact, seventy-one times in these verses, written to be sung, you see the musical instruction 'Selah'. This indicates a pause, a ceasing of the music, an interval of sorts to catch your breath and reflect. We tend to read right through them, but if you do pause and let the quiet sit there, it can be very powerful. It can also be very awkward if you are reading in public and don't warn people. I have had people trying to prompt me, offering me water, squirming and whispering, thinking I was having some sort of health episode simply because I had allowed a moment of quiet. I have learned to announce quiet moments now so no one panics.

 Learn

Learning to retreat in daily life

I have found you learn to be quiet by . . . being quiet!

I remember deciding I needed to learn more about this discipline of quiet by taking myself off to a local retreat centre for a personal self-guided retreat, and taking nothing at all with me so I could just enjoy the quiet. Enjoy! The first ten minutes were interminable and the rest of the day was not much better. Why had I done this to myself? What was I thinking of? I remembered what had prompted the visit.

I had watched a wonderful TV programme about a monastery[2] where several members of the public were invited to spend some weeks connecting with themselves and the quiet. In one episode the man visiting was spending time with a monk for what I thought would be a prayer time and some counselling. This was a man who had been very broken in his life. However, the monk offered very few words. I felt he was missing his opportunity to preach the gospel, or at least pray some words, and at one point the two men just sat together in silence and the monk looked with great love and acceptance on the man. It was the most powerful five minutes of TV I have ever seen. No one spoke. It went from awkward to intoxicating. The man who was visiting eventually began to sob and the presence of God was so evident I would not have been surprised if Jesus himself and a posse of angels hadn't stepped out of the screen into my room.

In quietness God had showed up.

So back to my silent retreat, or my silent restless wander around a retreat centre. What was I doing wrong? Did I need a monk? I had taken with me just one word that I felt God had given me. The word was 'delight'. I had decided to practise centring prayer with this one word. I now realize I was attempting to swim the Channel before learning to doggy paddle with water wings; the practice of quietness takes time.

So I wandered around. I ate all my snacks. I made copious cups of tea, I read every sign on every wall. I sat down, I stood up, I knelt, I walked, I tried to sit still and time dragged on.

I left the retreat centre many hours later feeling a complete failure. I had been silent, sure enough, but what had it proved and what had I gained? Nothing. Eventually my inner voice ran out of complaints and I lapsed into inner quiet as I drove home. The word 'delight' came into my mind. Then a strange thing happened. The very same views I had seen on the drive over suddenly became clear and beautiful to me, full of delight. So much so that I had to pull the car over and get out and walk by a river I had not even noticed passing before.

As I walked, the tears began to flow. Everything was so delightful. This tree. Delightful. The bird song. Delightful. The colours of the fading light. Delightful. I sat by the river, still and quiet at last, inside as well as outside, and the whisper of heaven, 'I delight in you, Ruth' filled my whole being.

What had happened? Should I have just stopped here on the way over and realized God was at the river more than the retreat centre? No. I think what had happened was the quietness had created a space, a quiet space where the delight that was already all around me could flood in. Due to the cluttered nature of my thoughts and the overactivity of my body, it just took all day for the quietness to settle in and the decluttering to make some room.

This is why I now try a little of this every day so that the quietness gets a chance to settle and be part of my everyday life.

Every now and then I hear him singing over me. He quiets me 'by his love'.

 **Get Active**

As well as the practice of quietness by actually being quiet, I have learned a lot from being quiet with others. I have learned to make sure people know that we are going to have some quiet together, and to make sure I scaffold it and don't leave people in quietness too long as it can be scary. However, in groups where we are committed to the practice of silence, we can spend twenty minutes sitting in quiet meditation without me fidgeting too much or needing to fill the silence with my words. I get out of practice easily with this one.

We also have a quiet room in every Renew space that is kept free of noise and chatter so that anyone can take themselves off for a moment of quiet and practise being at peace with themselves, and encounter God in the quiet. This is key also for our wellbeing, I believe. Many people have said how much easier it is to be quiet when in the company of others than when at home alone.

The idea of our quiet rooms is so that people can learn that silence need not be scary. As Christians we have a unique part to play in the wellbeing story in having spaces where solitude can be learned, as ultimately, this is the answer to combating loneliness. It may seem strange as it is obvious I am keen on community, but at some point in every life we are left alone with ourselves and this can be scary for some. How wonderful to have a space, then, that is shared yet is for silence. Just sitting in a room where others are also enjoying the quiet has taught me there is no need to fill every gap with the sound of my voice. What a relief to enjoy a quiet moment in the company of others so that when I am alone in the middle of the night and my head is playing tricks on me, I can remember what I learned in that quiet room, and be still in God's presence without fear.

> How wonderful to have a space, then, that is shared yet is for silence.

 Take Notice

I realized how powerful shared quiet can be, not in the context of a church, but in my previous life as a teacher of small children.

When I lost my voice, the doctor and occupational therapist had said I could return to work but had to take a voice break every hour for five minutes. This was easier said than done as a primary school teacher, but I was determined to get back to teaching so I came up with an idea. If a voice break was good for me, maybe it would be good for everyone. So instead of getting cover to leave the room, I explained my dilemma to the children who were very kind and understanding and together we came up with the hourly quiet moment idea.

Every hour on the hour I would shake a tambourine. Each child would collect their thinking book and pens and find a comfy cushion or corner. Then the timer would start or sometimes the quiet music, and every child, along with me, would take a five-minute voice break. We would each write or draw what we were thinking about, or just sit quietly and listen to the sounds around us.

Two things amazed me. One was how much the children loved the voice-break times and stuck to it. The second was how much more learning went on and the quality of it in the other fifty-five minutes. The time to reflect, to be quiet, to let our heads catch up with themselves was so vital, and we only happened on this truth through brokenness and failure.

Sadly, as my voice returned the quiet moments vanished and it all became a bit frenetic again. Why, oh why, I ask myself, can I not remember that the pauses are as vital as the learning, that the quiet is as important as the words?

Give

QUESTIONS

Do you find silence easy or hard? What helps or distracts you?

When have you found quiet times alone to be helpful? Describe a quiet peaceful moment in your life.

When have you practised quiet with others? How did it feel?

PRAYER

Lord who spoke out of the great silence
Draw me back into the stillness of the pre-created deep
And gently, please sing over me
Lull me again into peaceful sleep

Silence all my fears
Still my inner chatter
Let delight creep into every emptied space
And may I know again
The quieting of your love
and the whisper of your grace[3]

Resources

The Big Silence, BBC Two, 2010.

The Monastery, BBC Two, a documentary made in 2005. Or read about this in the book *Finding Sanctuary* by Father Christopher Jamison.[4]

R is for Renew

 **Connect**

Be transformed by the renewal of your mind . . . (Romans 12:2)

This is quite a key word for me. Obviously. I named a charity after it! To renew or make new again is at the very heart of what I long to see happen with wellbeing everywhere – what I think God wants to do with wellbeing everywhere. So I thought I would look into why I feel so strongly about this little word. To be honest, I love lots of words with the prefix 're'. There were many I could have chosen here: refresh, restore, redeem, recycle, reveal, repurpose, reflect. But all of these words lead me back to this key word: renew.

To make new again is what I believe the gospel is all about. God did not just keep on telling us how much we were spoiling the newness of creation, or our lives. Instead, he himself came and made all things new. In dying and rising again, Jesus made it possible for us to keep on being made new. Renewed.

> To make new again is what I believe the gospel is all about.

Let's look at three promises of renewal in the Bible.

The prophet Isaiah tells us in the beautiful passage in chapter 40 that if we 'wait for the LORD' we will 'renew [our] strength' (v. 31). There is talk of that feeling like we are rising up on eagles' wings or running forever and not getting tired. This idea of being renewed really appeals to me. I'm sure it does to you too. The thought that God can make our strength new again when it is all worn out, when we are all worn out, is a lovely one. It sounds like wellbeing, doesn't it?

But renew holds more than this wonderful promise of strength for me. It is not just a promise that if we wait on God he will renew us. There is even better news. As Jesus steps into view, we discover he doesn't even expect us to actively wait. He bridges the gap and steps into our world, bringing the chance of newness that we don't deserve or earn. He literally gives us new life.

In 2 Corinthians 4 Paul tells us that we are like clay jars with a treasure in them.

'Though outwardly we are wasting away, yet inwardly we are being renewed day by day' (v. 16, NIV).

How I love this image! This is what renewal feels like to me. It is why I love the cup thing so much. It feels so often that the pot that I am is cracked and broken and fading away, yet inwardly I can know a complete sense of being new again, of new life coursing through me. I often don't feel any less outwardly weary; I still need to sleep and eat well and exercise. I spent years misunderstanding this favourite passage and thinking that if I just trusted God I could overwork and treat my body with disrespect and it wouldn't matter because I was being renewed inside. In many ways this is true, yet I forgot my inside and my outside are indeed the same person, connected, and that what affects my mind affects my body and vice versa.

I believe this passage is an invitation to wholeness. It is an invitation to understand that when one day the outer tent[1] wears out, our inner lives, our spirits will carry on; that the new life he gives us is not dependent on us being OK. It is therefore genuinely 'OK not to be OK' and still have his renewing going on. It makes sense of the times I have marvelled at the glory shining out of a dying or suffering friend. It gives me great hope that even when I don't care well for myself, he is still renewing me from the inside out. This is what salvation looks like for me. It is a one-off act of love and forgiveness and renewing, but it is also a day-by-day movement of God towards making me new every day, until one day the ultimate renewing will happen. In the last book of the Bible it says that he will make 'all things new' (Rev. 21:5).

So the whole of creation is precious and not dispensable. It is all being made new. Caring for the planet is vital to our wellbeing too. This is a renewing planet. It matters how we care for it. It matters in itself and it matters to our wellbeing.

As if this wasn't good news enough, there is a third aspect of renewing I want to share that has been vital for my wellbeing. In his letter to the Romans, Paul tells us to be 'transformed by the renewing of [our] mind' (Rom. 12:2, NIV). This is great news for me. The battle rages in my mind. This is where the thought processes can floor me or lift me up. So the idea that this is where God is at work renewing me is great; this is where real transformation will happen for me.

I like the Five Ways to Wellbeing that the New Economics Foundation[2] outlined after their research into wellbeing – connecting, learning, getting active, taking notice and giving all help us attend to wellbeing. I like them as simple ways to look after our wellbeing but I have also found them to be a good structure for helping us dig deeper into each letter of the alphabet on this wellbeing journey. Advice from mental health professionals is often about changing an outer behaviour and an inner change will follow.[3] But I *love* the promise in these words of God that he is committed to renewing me from the inside even when I am powerless to do anything at all.

This 'renewing of [my] mind', renewing of my very life, renewing of my strength, is something the Spirit of God is doing in me. I can join in with this or fight it and try to do it all myself. I have found it better to hand over the control to God who loves and cares for me so well. He does not just patch me up, make the best of a bad job – he makes all things, including me, new.

 Learn

The slow work of making things new

I have watched enough TV programmes to know that restoration and renewing is not a quick process. I have seen people use up all their savings, all their energy and all their time to rebuild a few walls and make good a rotting building. The idea that I am the restoration project makes me understand how long this might take. God is fully committed to the timescale on this. I'm not so sure I always am. I do love a quick fix! My parents remind me sometimes of the clothes I made myself in my teens where the hems were stuck with sticky tape as I got fed up before I finished. Or my husband will tell you about the kitchen tiles I painted and the unpainted patch he discovered years later behind the microwave that I couldn't be bothered to move.

So I need help with the slow process of renewing. If renewing is God's work, how can I join in? Let's look at the three areas again and see if there's anything I can do without trying to rush God.

Firstly, God renews my strength. Here is a call to wait actively. What does that look like? For me the web I weave of waiting on God looks like all the simple habits I have already described in these pages. Holding a cup, sitting still, meditating, a rhythm of prayer, reading the Bible, having a hobby, being part of a community. All these things are like the threads a spider spins. In themselves they are quite fragile and do not hold the nutrition the spider needs. When I talk about these habits I am not saying they give me wellbeing, but that they allow me to grab hold of the wellbeing that I believe God brings to me. *Shalom* is not something I create but something that is already out there and in keeping my waiting habits, I grab hold of it.

So when I am weak and lacking strength I rest, I choose better, healthier food and exercise, I ask for help and in these waiting habits I encounter God's *shalom*. He would still be good and all around me if I didn't do these things, and eventually I would realize this in some other way, but in choosing to attend to my wellbeing with simple habits I get myself ready to welcome his wellbeing that is all around me.

Secondly, being made new because of the cross of Jesus, the new life he offers, this is all a gift. Surely there is no way I can join in here? I'm sure you have received a gift at some point in your life. To be able to receive it you first needed to put down what was in your hands, to turn to face the person gifting you, and to be willing to receive it. What a sad thought that someone has got you a precious gift, wrapped lovingly, and is holding it out to you and you have arms full of rubbish on the way to the bin and say you can't let go, don't have time, and you won't open your hands to receive what has been bought for you.

This image is the one I think of when I am being offered life over and over again by the God of new beginnings. All I do is say yes to him each day in my habits of prayer and surrender. He renews my life.

Thirdly, being renewed in my mind requires me to join in by deciding what to think about. I didn't know I could do this until I was ill and so imprisoned by every worry and fear; I thought I was at the mercy of every thought that passed through my head. As I began the new art of meditation on Psalms, I realized that I couldn't stop myself thinking anxious thoughts but I could replace a thought with a better one. I found the simple act of taking one phrase from God's Word that is always good and true and placing this at the centre of my thoughts was like taking every thought 'captive' (2 Cor. 10:5). What a great description Paul uses here. I can picture my thoughts running round my head firing indiscriminately at my peace and generally causing chaos. Then I see myself placing the words of meditation in the centre of my head and it lassoing every thought that is causing damage and pulling it into the safe embrace of the truth. Taking thoughts captive, making them obedient to the Word. It helps a visual thinker like me to understand how I can join in with what God is doing simply by placing a good and true saying in my head.

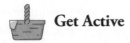 **Get Active**

In this section, which looks at what we can do together to help us grasp the word 'renew', I want to be a bit practical. The word 'renew' makes me think of all the amazing TV programmes I love to watch where old, battered, worn-out objects are taken and restored or made new. I love everything that shows you how to repair or renew, to upcycle things that would otherwise be thrown away. I have a very close relationship with charity shops and like nothing better than looking around other people's discarded items and finding something I can give new life to. I can't say all my attempts are successful; sometimes the poor object had a better chance in its old life. I can remember one summer finding old jumpers and woollens in charity shops when on holiday in the Isle of Man and making them into felt by washing on a high heat and drying quickly. Then I made each jumper into a bag.

As my children pointed out, it was pretty pointless as I then ended up giving all the bags back to the charity shop. One of my darling kids asked if the next step was to buy some bags and make them into jumpers. Children keep you humble!

But for me, the process of upcycling, of repairing, of giving a new lease of life to an otherwise throwaway item is exhilarating and life-giving. I think this is because it mirrors that process of God making me new. He takes me from the scrap heap and he makes me new.

> Giving a new lease of life to an otherwise throwaway item is exhilarating and life-giving . . . it mirrors that process of God making me new.

So in our Renew centres we love to take old things and upcycle them. I would love to see every Renew space having a meaningful relationship with a charity shop. We can take objects that are donated but need some love and make them new so that they make more money for charity. This gives us as a community a sense of purpose as well as being good for our wellbeing, just to get creative with an old object.

I have seen some beautiful upcycling and restoration projects in our centres and long to see even more of this, as I believe it to be a prophetic image of what we are doing.

 Take Notice

In the very early days of renew37, this idea of making new or renewing was really strong with me. Every scrap of furniture with the exception of a few tables was either donated, bought from a charity shop or made from scratch. This meant that we spent lots of time in those preparation months in a gazebo on the pavement outside the property with a piece of sandpaper or a paintbrush in hand. This was a moment when the community could begin to come together to see the new emerge from the old and battered.

I can remember asking for only wooden chairs, even though it may have been better to get stacking plastic chairs, and there was an offer to buy these. But to me, it was clear and important that every item could be constantly renewed. There was also the fact that we shared the space with the tea house next door and they had the wooden chair theme already, so we wanted to work in harmony with that. The beauty of wooden chairs donated from people's garages was that each was a little unique and could be sanded back to its original wood. Under the layers of dirt and varnish there was the purity of what the chair had been made from.

Then we could choose a beautiful colour of chalk paint and make these old, discarded chairs into works of art. A word of caution here. We found out the hard way that you can't just use any old paint and hope for the best. Often to get a great finish, there was some spending on good materials required. One chair was painted hastily in some leftover gloss and never dried properly. We only realized this when the tea house was using the space and an irate customer stood up to find her new trousers covered in white, sticky paint. We replaced the trousers. There was no other way to make them new! This did make me think that in the restoration of our lives, God only uses the most expensive materials. The cost of our renewing was the life of his Son. Not cheap.

After painting, rubbing wax lovingly into the finished chair to protect it felt like a meditation in itself. Then within the year it all needed doing again.

This renewing is an iterative process. That is, it needs repeating over and over. I love this about renewing old objects and I love this about God's renewing of my life.

Give

QUESTIONS

What renewing projects have you been involved in or enjoyed watching?

Do you have habits that help you join in with God's renewing of you?

When you think of God renewing the planet or renewing community, what actions come to mind?

PRAYER

Renew me
Great restorer of my soul
Strip back the years of wear and tear
And make me whole

Renew my mind
Renew my strength
Renew my hope
Renew this breath
Renew the world
Bring life from death
So I will wait, take captive every thought
And I'll emerge renewed, restored
Handmade
And by my Maker
Rebought

Resources

The Repair Shop, BBC One. This is a TV programme where a team of experts take old, precious items and carefully restore them to their former glory. I would love to see a version of this in every Renew centre (although maybe with fewer experts!): https://www.bbc.co.uk/programmes/b08l581p

S is for Simple

 **Connect**

Everyone who loves has been born of God and knows God . . .
God is love.

(1 John 4:7–8, NIV)

I love the word 'simple'. It is one of the words that forms my rule of life. It is not a new word but to me, it was a life-changing idea when applied to my wellbeing.

I remember being at Ffald-y-Brenin retreat centre in South Wales at a low time in my life, seeking healing and answers. I sat in the lovely little prayer room, cave-shaped and full of the presence of God, and heard the word used in a repeated prayer. 'Lord, keep us in the beautiful attitudes, joyful, simple, and gentle.'[1]

That word 'simple' had never come to mind for me when I considered my life in Christ. As a lifelong follower of Jesus, nothing seemed simple. There were lots of demands on my time, lots of expectations and judgement flying around. Lots of meetings and lots of joy. But simplicity was not something I was familiar with. This was not language I thought belonged in a place where there was a world to be saved and a mysterious but loving God to be known.

But I was so drawn to the word that I began to look for it in the Bible. I was disappointed to find in the Old Testament it was mostly used as the opposite of wise. A simple person was someone lacking in wisdom. For example, in Proverbs a simple person is someone who believes anything anyone tells them.[2] There are a few exceptions to this but generally I came away with the impression that this was not a word for the godly. Then I looked into the New Testament Greek and found there was not much more here. I was about to turn away from this captivating word when I began to spot the idea of simplicity leaping out at me in every reading of Scripture. The idea was of purity, of single-minded, wholehearted openness to God. The idea was of a singularity of purpose and vision, not a complex mess of purposes.

Because I am so keen on actual words and I was looking for the English word 'simple' or 'simplicity', I nearly missed the embodiment of simplicity which is Jesus himself. His single-minded life of compassion and love given for us led him to keep to simplicity at every level. He had 'nowhere to lay his head' (Luke 9:58). In Matthew 10, he sends the disciples out with nothing but their message. He praises the woman who simply gives everything (Luke 21:1–4). And in his death on the cross, he set his face towards Jerusalem (Luke 9:51) and endured terrible suffering 'for the joy that was set before him' (Heb. 12:2). He had a simple heart of love and made a simple sacrifice for us. Simple does not mean easy and it has layers of depth to it. But 'simple' can mean to devote oneself entirely to a course of action.

This vision of simplicity, this invitation to the simple life has led me to some new thoughts and practices that I am only just settling into.

Learn

Ruthless inner decluttering

Learning simplicity has not been simple! Now, there's an irony. To live simply, unattached to stuff. To own less and be more grateful for what I have. To be single-minded in what I get involved in and not overstretch myself. This all sounds easy but simple is not easy. It is actually quite difficult. Complexity is much easier. To allow lots of people and things and ideas to clutter my life means I don't have to choose. I just let it all happen. But it does not make for simplicity!

> Learning simplicity has not been simple . . . Complexity is much easier.

I learned a lot by reading a book that is not at all from a Christian perspective, but it gets at good wellbeing truth. *Think Simple* by Ken Segall is subtitled 'How smart leaders defeat complexity'. This author looks at a variety of businesses where the quest for simplicity has meant great success.[3] This was an eye-opener to me. I had always thought success in any area of life meant change and creativity and working harder. But this author's fascination with certain successful business leaders was the way in which they could simplify the product right down to just a few items, and then make them and sell them really well.

This is not the only way to learn simplicity, but it does seem that to simplify means less, not more. It means asking questions about what you are really passionate about, what you really need, and then getting rid of anything that clutters that vision. This can apply in your wardrobe and your mind.

I had to learn how to let go of all the many pioneering and exciting ideas that flew round my head. These were the enemies of simplicity for me. I had an idea a minute for change and life, and the poor church I led were on a white-knuckle ride at times because of my need for change and adventure. I found the Enneagram helpful here.[4] This enables you to see your own personality type, but there is lots of room for growth, and it doesn't label you.

I also learned a lot working with a spiritual director on my rule of life.[5] This is not a set of rules, but, like a plant sometimes needs a structure to guide its growth, it is a set of practices or words that help you shape simplicity in your life. It helped me find and stick to what God was calling me to. As I am a rule-keeper and a bit legalistic, I found it helpful not to have a list of things to do for my rule of life. Some people have a list of when they will go on retreat, rest, study etc. I had three words, gleaned from the Ffald-y-Brenin daily office: simple, joyful, gentle. This is my rule of life which I revisit monthly.

 **Get Active**

It is really hard to stick to simplicity in such a complex world. Our Renew spaces are super-simple when they start, but it is easy to get taken over by the agendas of others who want to try to fix people or do prayer ministry or counselling services. These all have their place, but the beauty of a Renew space is that you can signpost to extra help, and keep the Renew space a place where all are equal. It is strength-based, not looking for weaknesses.

To help maintain this simplicity we ask each centre to sign an agreement as follows:

Family Agreement

Welcome to the Renew Wellbeing family.

We are so glad you have decided to open a renew space.

Please could you read and sign the following family agreement and use it to train hosts and remind your church family about what having a Renew space means.

If you are happy to sign up to these values and make every effort to maintain them, then do feel free to use the Renew Wellbeing logo and to join the renew wellbeing online family. You are also most welcome to join us at our annual gatherings and retreats (see website).[6]

Signing up to becoming a Renew space means you are part of a national movement and as such it is important to keep our values strong. This agreement means you are happy to work with the Renew team and share what you are learning through our review process.

1. Being Present

We agree to maintain a well-hosted, welcoming, inclusive, quiet shared space with a café feel that is open to all and overtly inclusive of anyone with mental health issues.

We agree to co-produce all activities, welcoming others to share hobbies.

We agree to display and use as a guide the Five Ways to Wellbeing to ensure a rounded, healthy variety of activities.

We agree to be present consistently at the times we have agreed to be open, with at least two hosts present at each session.

2. Being in Partnership

We agree to find, befriend and work with a member of the local mental health team.

We agree to learn from and listen to those with professional skills and/or lived experience of mental ill health.

3. Being Prayerful

We agree to establish simple rhythms of prayer that are open and accessible to all in a space separate from the main café space but if possible attached to it.

We agree to use simple patterns that are easy to understand for all abilities and ages and to invite/welcome anyone to short prayer sessions.

We agree to keep a quiet space available to anyone and to use the space ourselves as hosts and organizers, to allow people to sit in God's presence quietly.

This simple agreement is re-signed every year.

Every three months there is a review with one of the team of coordinators to answer simple questions around the three principles, such as:

How is it going being present in your space?
How are your partnerships with mental health services developing?
How are the prayer times going?
What are you learning that may help other centres?
How can we help you?

Each week there are opportunities to connect nationally and locally online.

Three times a year there are opportunities to connect with all the other centres at an online event.

There is an ongoing Facebook group for hosts to share good practice.

In all these ways and more, we want to help keep things simple.

I often refer to the review process as watering and weeding, sometimes as pruning. It is always a cultivation image and it often results in growth.

Simplicity takes a lot of work to maintain.

 Take Notice

Another day at Renew. The kettle is on. The activities are out on the tables. Not too much, as it can feel over fussy. A few colouring sheets at one table, a jigsaw at the next, a game of dominoes ready to be played, some art materials ready for any who fancy painting. There is a stillness over the place as the hosts potter around preparing the space, writing today's activities on the chalkboard, checking the refreshments area is stocked up, tidying the leaflets that signpost to other good wellbeing activities in the town.

The clock tells us it is time for prayer and one host wanders through to the prayer room, propping the door open and sits quietly for a moment or two before starting the prayer time with the one or two who have arrived. The other host sits at the table near the door and begins to quietly colour in, her head and heart praying with those she can hear in the quiet room working through the psalm, her eyes on the door ready to greet and welcome those who wander by.

There is a hush, a stillness and those who arrive talk in calm voices as they greet each other and make their cuppa for the morning. Some wander into the prayer space, one or two take a look in and decide to come back later when there are more people to hide them.

The tables begin to fill up. One gets out their knitting. Another reads the paper and two others take their cuppas to the dominoes table and begin to play. The folk in the prayer room wander out one by one, get their drink and join those already making themselves at home. Some potter off to the shops or to work. Others arrive. The morning passes calmly; cakes arrive from somewhere.

Suddenly the host leading prayer is wandering round with the reminder that the Lord's Prayer will be prayed in five minutes. Everyone comments on how fast the time has flown by. Some get up and make their way through to the quiet room, others continue what they are doing but the volume goes down other people say their goodbyes and head off with a promise to pop in later in the week.

Soon the sound of sentence prayers leaks through from the quiet room; the peace descends again. All is calm. More folk arrive, and the kettle boils again. Those who were praying begin to join tables and get out their lunches, some pop next door and get a sandwich and one to share. Laughter fills the air. The gentleman showing us how to make bird boxes arrives and sets up on the corner table. Rachel from the mental health team pops in with a friend for a chat and a cuppa.

The simple rhythm of the day continues as it will do tomorrow and the next day. Simplicity day in, day out, year in, year out. Simple, steady, calming, peaceful, beautiful.

Give

QUESTIONS

What does simplicity look like in your life?

What constant rhythms do you have for your wellbeing?

What stops simplicity in your life?

PRAYER

A poem in lockdown, May 2020

I am learning
The catharsis of the heart
Needs heat
Before the purifying starts

I am learning
That the needs I thought were key
Were wants
Not needs
Not me

I am learning
That the things I really miss
Are not things at all
But dear ones
To hug and kiss

I am learning
That I needed less
Than I thought
To be content
Wellbeing can't be bought

I am learning
That as the outer life
Locks down
The inner life expands
To wear compassion's crown

I am learning
That I'm not OK
Every day
I don't like Zoom
I like real rooms

I am learning
That even though
He is enough
I sometimes miss
The other stuff

I am learning
I love the world
I need my friends
I am learning
To live with less
Until this ends

I am learning
That as I skim off old desires
I see you, Lord
With clearer eyes
I am learning

Resources

Richard Rohr, *Just This*. A beautiful little book with simple reflections.

Ffald-y-Brenin retreat centre:
https://ffald-y-brenin.org/

$\boxed{\text{T}}$ is for Thanks

 **Connect**

Give thanks . . . (Psalm 118:1)

The letter T is for thanks. This won't surprise anyone. In an alphabet of wellbeing, gratitude had to make the cut. A good friend of mine who has been both a psychiatrist and a priest and who advises me on all things Renew Wellbeing, has told me on more than one occasion that using the Five Ways to Wellbeing leaves out the vital sixth way – of gratitude. I insist that gratitude is the attitude with which all the other five ways could be viewed, but to tell people to be more grateful when they are down feels too hard. It's a regular discussion we enjoy in our adventure to find out what wellbeing actually is.

So, what I wouldn't want to do with this word is make anyone feel like I sometimes felt when I was unwell or struggling with low mood: like I should be more grateful. This can shut down honest dialogue and make someone feel guilty. The whole concept of thankfulness has been used in child-rearing and church settings alike to try to help people with their emotional state and has more often than not had the opposite effect to that which was intended.

But there is no doubt that the Bible is full of instruction to be thankful. Psalms 95, 100, 106, 107 to name but a few suggest thanksgiving is the way to enter God's presence. Certainly I am learning how powerful this can be. But is there a way to understand thankfulness that is gentler on the weary ones and less relentlessly positive?

The word '*yadah*' in Hebrew, often translated as thanks or praise, is a physical expression of extending the hand towards someone as a way of confessing where a good thing has come from. It is a confession, an act of the will to recognize the source of a good gift. It is not a feeling first and foremost, but an action that represents a timeless truth. I find this helps. When I am being instructed to give thanks to God, I am not being told to feel more grateful or to stop moaning and complaining. Even a cursory reading of the Psalms leads me to believe it's OK to do both: praise and lament.

But thankfulness is a confession of faith. It is a recognition that there is a God and it isn't me. It is a statement of fact that God is the creator and author of all that is good.

When we give thanks to someone else for a gift, it is because there is a truth there that one person has given something to the other and the thanks is the recognition of the act. It has less to do with feeling and more to do with a statement of what is happening. Of course we can feel thankful. But we have all known times in our lives when we have said 'thank you' and not felt it. It was still the best thing to do and made a difference to the moment and the relationship.

As we give thanks, something happens within us. The truth begins to settle in me as I thank God each day before I begin to ask him for stuff. I thank him for who he is, and then what he has done, and gradually all the things I thought were so vital for my wellbeing begin to take their proper place.

To give thanks as a decision, as a habit, as a choice has been mind-changing for me.

To give thanks as a decision, as a habit, as a choice has been mind-changing for me.

 Learn: daily bread

The reverse shopping list

I am learning to be thankful. I have been learning it since I was a little girl and my parents brought me up to say 'please' and 'thank you' a lot! I find it so easy to forget all the many things I have and only see the one thing I think I need. So often, especially when I was unwell, my prayers became a desperate cry for God to fix the one thing wrong with me with no acknowledgement of all the things that were right that day. My shopping-list prayers for all the people and situations I was concerned for could make prayer more like worrying with my eyes shut than encountering God's peaceful presence.

By engaging with the rhythms of prayer, I am learning to be honest about my feelings, ask for what is needed, but also to list the things I am thankful for. It becomes a little like a reverse shopping list. A game to list as many things in a minute or two each day that I might otherwise take for granted. Air, shelter, food, warmth, a new day, etc. When I use the Psalm 103 prayer, 'Bless the Lord, O my soul, and forget not all his benefits' I list the things I am thankful for. In the Lord's Prayer, when we ask for daily bread,[1] we first pause and thank him for actual bread and food and simple things. In the prayer of Examen[2] at the end of the day, we rewind or replay the day looking for things to be thankful for. I find this a great way to get off to sleep – it

225

is like counting sheep for me. It is so easy to finish the day berating yourself for what went wrong, replaying scenarios and conversations. If I occupy my mind with a reverse shopping list of thanks, I find a lot of small details to be thankful for and I soon drop off. I am not saying I always remember to do this. I wish I did!

> If I occupy my mind with a reverse shopping list of thanks, I find a lot of small details to be thankful for.

When this is shared, it can be fun – opening up a time to name all the things we are thankful for that day. It is usually the most vocal part of the shared prayer time.

It is not mind control or relentless positivity. It is still sitting alongside lament and complaint and honest feelings, but there are always things to make us thankful if we pause and list them. I am finding it to be a good habit. I need to do it three times a day because I am prone towards complaint and self-criticism so much.

 **Get Active**

To give thanks together is a powerful thing. I love to share these habits of prayer with others. During the pandemic lockdown in 2020 and 2021 I began a prayer time online every morning, and what a joy that was to hear what others were thankful for even on my barren days. Together we reminded each other of things like shelter and porridge and forgiveness. Together we filled our little empty rooms at home with the sound of his name each day. It kept me going, this shared thankfulness. That's what Renew centres are all about. Of course, we then lamented and asked God to intervene. We confessed sin and blessed each other. But we always started with thanks. What a wellbeing-giving discipline.

I love the way our communities of wellbeing, be they family, friendship, church or Renew space, are beautiful and life-giving when they are full of thankfulness for and to each other. It has been so lovely when people have taken time to encourage me and thank me. At any point in our life, to have someone say 'thank you' does something for our souls. This is why the habit of thanking people in a little note or email is something I am trying to do more. It is too easy to think a thankful thought but never follow it through with thanks.

In our Renew spaces, we try to allow everyone to give and receive so that everyone becomes recipients of thanks as well as givers of thanks. There is something life-giving about being able to do something for someone else rather than being done unto all the time. I think this 'thankfulness' word links to the fifth way to wellbeing which is giving. I believe one of the secrets of the Renew movement is that the church steps down from the power position of doing all the giving and allows others to serve and give. Anyone can make a cuppa, share a hobby, bring a skill. In this way everyone in the place hears 'thank you' and feels the joy of having helped someone else.

Many folk have reported to me that this is what they like about our spaces. The church is not in the driving seat. It is not yet another place where people feel they are using a service for which they need to be thankful. It is also a place where everyone can learn to give and share and receive thanks. We foster thankfulness among all who attend and it is amazing what that does to our sense of entitlement and comparison, which can so often leave us feeling dissatisfied and left out.

 **Take Notice**

I am so thankful at the moment for what is happening in Scotland. I want to take a moment to recognize it and give thanks to God for it. I can be so determined to see a Renew centre on every corner that I don't take enough time to stop and see what is right in front of me.

For a long time after Renew Wellbeing started we had no interest coming from Scotland. I was asked to speak at the Baptist Union of Scotland conference in July 2020, mid-pandemic. It was a lovely online event and I thought no more about it.

Then the emails started pinging in. One after another, Scottish churches were describing adventures they had already started that seemed very like Renew. It was such a delight to hear the feedback from my simple words at the conference, and to hear the eagerness.

So I tentatively offered in the January of 2021, as my book *Slow Down, Show Up and Pray* was released, that I would run a book group-style, two-session training for any churches interested. I imagined ten or twelve folk huddling round a book or two on a screen and maybe one or two Renew centres issuing from it.

I was overwhelmed when more than eighty people from all over Scotland attended the first two sessions and I had to re-run the sessions for those who missed the deadline, and another seventy-plus people came to the second training. With the seeds in the ground I sat back and waited. Soon, churches began contacting me for discussions and to get signed up to run Renew spaces.

This had all taken me by surprise, so much so that I had no coordinator for Scotland as I did for other parts of the UK, and I found myself taking on this delightful role as the network in Scotland grew.

The sheer speed of it made me dizzy and I could do nothing but thank God who had gone before me, was doing all the work and was reminding me that this was well and truly his work, his idea and his responsibility.

My job? To have a thankful heart.

Give

QUESTIONS

Do you find it easier to give or receive? Why?

What's one of the best gifts you have ever received or given?

What makes it hard for you to ask for help?

PRAYER

As a prayer I could not write one as beautiful as this one:

> Thou that hast given so much to me give me one thing more, a grateful heart: not thankful when it pleaseth me, as if Thy blessings had spare days, but such a heart whose pulse may be Thy praise.
>
> George Herbert[3]

Resources

Barbara Brown Taylor, *An Altar in the World.*
This amazing lady writes so beautifully about almost everything, including gratitude.
Read anything by Barbara Brown Taylor. It is like honey.

U is for Unite

 **Connect**

Love one another . . . (John 15:12)

This word 'unite' has been hijacked somewhat here in the UK by workers' unions and football fans. To hear the cry 'United' makes me think more of a famous team of players than of a spiritual truth undergirding my wellbeing. But I am coming to believe that this is a key part of anyone's wellbeing. To be united with God, with oneself and with others really helps with wellbeing. In fact, you could say it is part of the meaning of the word '*shalom*'.

God himself is united. The concept of the Trinity has been important for my grasp of wellbeing. Father, Son and Spirit: three in one means that all his creation reflects that sense of unity. We all crave this oneness, need this oneness.

I want to look at what the Bible says about our oneness with God but also our unity within ourselves and then with each other. Usually any talks I have heard about being united go straight to how we need to work together and love each other. This is vital in the wellbeing movement. God commands a blessing (Ps. 133:1–3) where there is unity between people.

But for me to unite with others, I am finding I need to know the solidity and identity of being united with God himself and then to unite within myself. If I skip straight to uniting with others without working on unity in myself, I find I quickly try to bend others to what I want, or to control them. I can become needy for the attention and the compassion of others and upset if I don't get it. I can put too much of my own sense of identity in how I help, relate to or am seen by others. In short, unity with others defines me rather than it being something that springs out of a sense of unity that is already there in God's nature and within me.

> If I skip straight to uniting with others without working on unity in myself, I find I quickly try to bend others to what I want.

In John 17, Jesus is praying for us. Imagine – we get to hear God talking within himself, Son to Father by the Spirit about you and me! This feels like a prayer we can learn a lot about this word 'unite' from.

In this beautiful prayer, Jesus prays for his disciples present and future, so that's us. He says this:

> I have given them the glory that you gave me, that they may be one as we are one – I in them and you in me – so that they may be brought to complete unity. Then the world will know that you sent me and have loved them even as you have loved me.[1]

Isn't this beautiful? And it is so clear that unity is what Jesus is all about and what he really wants for us. It ends with the world knowing we are his disciples because of our unity, but it starts with Jesus being in the Father and sharing his glory. Everything we see in one member of the Trinity we see in all three. This wonderful mystery of a triune God has had me debating and puzzling for years. These days I prefer wonder and awe and open-mouthed fascination to great arguments and debates. But I still search Scripture often for more hints at the glory of the three in one. When I am battling with my need for others and trying to sit quietly on my own I often remind myself before I get too harsh with my self-criticism that I am made in the image of a relational God, and that's why I crave company and love.

So back to this glorious prayer of Jesus'. After we are completely clear about his own oneness and sense of unity, he states that we are part of that too. He is in us and we are in him. Amazing. This is what happens when we simply repent, turn round, face him and ask him to forgive and live in us. United with him. One in him.

There is much imagery in the Bible around marriage. Two becoming one. United. This is the comparison God uses to speak of his relationship with his church.[2] There is a whole book, the Song of Songs, which uses the language of lovers. Many would say this is only about two human beings in love but I read it as a love letter from heaven to us too. These are verses we used to giggle over in the back row of church during a boring sermon. When read as an expression of God's love and desire for unity with us in the light of this prayer by Jesus in John 17, they seem less funny and more wonderful. What an amazing fact that fills me with a sense of wellbeing when I spend any time at all pondering it! God himself unites with me, with us. He chooses me, he desires unity with me. So much does he crave this oneness with me, with all creation, that he pays the ultimate price of his own life so that a way is opened up for this complete face-to-face unity to happen.

To unite with Christ, the action of being united with the God of the whole universe, holds within it all wellbeing for me. It means that whatever happens in the circumstances of my life, nothing and no one can separate me from him or his love, which is indeed all I need anyway.[3] This is why I need my faith so much. Without this unity with God, I don't know how I would have any wellbeing. It is why I have been so keen to learn all I can from those without faith, to try to understand their point of view and grasp how they live in wellbeing without this bigger story to which I am so united. It is why, if I am honest, I want every person I encounter to meet the God who loves them too. But I do know that there is much to learn, new perspectives that enrich this simple view. I am learning to listen to the views of others. It doesn't threaten my faith, it makes me more awestruck that God reveals himself to his beloved creation in so many ways.

> To be united with God means I can begin to be united within myself.

To be united with God means I can begin to be united within myself.

 Learn

The cappuccino life

The realization that is dawning on me over these last few years of the wellbeing adventure is that unity is needed in my own heart. The psalmist talks of having an 'undivided heart' (Ps. 86:11, NIV). It is taking me some time to understand that this is what is needed in me for real wellbeing to flow. Wellbeing as a translation of the word '*shalom*' holds within it the sense of all things coming together, whole. I have always understood this to refer to not having any bad stuff in there, to needing to be completely pure, and this has felt unmanageable. Whenever I lose my sense of peace, it is often because I have conflicting emotions. I am sad and weary as well as joyful and fulfilled, and I feel I have to pretend all the negatives away. I have always thought an 'undivided heart' would be one that is wholly full of joy and peace and positives.

The gradual dawning as we pray Psalm 103 each day is that I need to bring 'all that is within me' (v. 1). This is what we pray as we tell our souls to 'bless the LORD' at the start of each day. We say that we bring 'all that is within' us but then I realize that I am only bringing the acceptable thoughts and parts of me. I so often have metaphorically checked in my baggage at the door, entered his presence and then left again, picking up all my baggage on the way out so I can sort it out myself. To be united in heart is becoming a habit I now try to engage in each morning as I meditate. I take a look within and name what is there. Sometimes there is fear and worry alongside the joy of a new day. What am I saying? There is always fear and worry in there, if I am being completely honest. So each day I bring it with me as I begin to bless his name. Letting the fears see the truth and the light does put them in perspective. When I manage to do this honestly, it brings my heart to a place of unity within itself. I am accepting all parts of me, not judging and deciding for God what is acceptable. 'All that is within' me can then begin to bless him. I call it my 'cappuccino life'. A cappuccino has a mix of bitter coffee, frothy milk and chocolate on the top. All are needed. The mix makes the drink. Joy and sorrow can co-exist.

United in heart. Undivided. This will not happen until I am face to face with him one day. But the rest of my life gives me lots of practice opportunities.

 **Get Active**

When I unite with him and become more united within myself, I do find it easier to judge less and accept more. To unite with others then becomes a privilege rather than a power struggle.

We do need each other, but I find it all works better when I don't come to others as needy. 'In need' is different. I can have a need and be able to voice it honestly when I have recognized it, as I bring my united heart. But when I become needy, that is, I think, 'someone else has what I need and should be able to fix me, help me', then I get easily disappointed.

Jesus' prayer for us is that we will be one as he is one with the Father and the Spirit.[4] This sort of unity has each bringing something to the relationship, a mutuality not a dependence. An interdependence, not individuality.

This is the sort of unity we practise and seek in our Renew spaces. We invite each person to come and bring all of who they are. OK and not OK parts. When we learn to accept and be united to God and to accept and unite within our own hearts, I find it less vital that I have to make sure everyone else is OK and united within themselves. It isn't that I don't care. I care deeply. Compassion means that we choose a hard path when we want to be united. We will feel each other's pain. We will be affected by it. But what I am learning is that I can be united to others just as they are, not try to make them fit around who I think they should be, or panic when they are not OK and feel that unity with them requires me to make them OK.

The whole concept of unity is so important in our Renew spaces. Not only do we co-produce so that we can unite healthily without power dynamics across the room from hosts to regulars – all are equal; mental health is a leveller; we all have it – but we are finding how much this wellbeing language unites us across our churches and denominations, across our communities and services. We all need wellbeing, but most of us don't really have it. We are all learning together. This is a uniting language. It is why I am so keen on it – no one is the ultimate authority on wellbeing. We are all learners. We unite and bring what we carry and each has a part in the wellbeing community.

When people unite together around wellbeing, amazing things happen.

 Take Notice

Some of our Renew centres are wonderful examples of unity in practice.

Renew 5 Northallerton. This is a great example where five churches put money, time and effort into one pot to open a space all week to their community. As part of the Living Rooms project, Renew 5 provides a still point at the heart of all the amazing community services on offer.

Renew 169 Towcester. This project was initiated by Laura from the Baptist church, but very soon became a community-led project with the churches at the heart. The training for this was so memorable for me. Usually I arrived at a church building where a few Christians who already had an inkling of what they were coming to have gathered. We pray; I introduce the Renew idea; we pray some more.

This time I arrived at a pub. Ushered into an upper room, I was met by around thirty folk from the churches and community all keen to learn about Renew. Lovely. But it became obvious fairly quickly they were not all speaking the same language with regards to faith. I really wasn't sure how the training for a place based on prayer would work out.

I excused myself and stood in one of the toilet cubicles and prayed what I call my 'Mr Benn' prayer. *Mr Benn* was a children's TV show when I was young where the lead character would go into a cubicle and would be transported to an adventure depending on what outfit the shopkeeper had given him to wear. It's a great watch! Anyway, I prayed that God would re-clothe me for this new adventure and show me how to bring the full message of Renew Wellbeing to such a mixed crowd.

I entered the room and God took over. I explained that this was unashamedly Christian and that prayer was a major component, but that I would run through the being present and being in partnership parts of the training first and then we could take a short break in case anyone wanted to leave, and I would end with the prayer rhythms.

At the break no one moved. Everyone stayed. The prayer training was the most powerful moment I have ever had when delivering it. The sense of God's presence in the pub was tangible. No one had a problem with prayer as a key element of this. The only question at the end was, 'When can we start and where shall we do it?'

Someone suggested an empty shop unit on the high street. So we prayed together, this group of those who spoke the language of church and those who had never prayed before. Laura and I wandered out onto the high street and took a photo in front of the empty shop and I went home marvelling at what had just happened.

The next day Laura rang to tell me they had been offered the shop rent-free for three months and could I help them get started straight away? Remarkable. God loves unity. The story continued with a great team and the council offering to pay the rent after the initial period of three months had ended.

This is still a fantastic community project now with a full-time paid manager.

Renew 23 Purley. It was sweltering as I arrived at Purley Baptist Church that summer's evening to talk to what I thought would be a few folk from the churches in Purley. The room was full and the enthusiasm levels were high. It soon transpired that these were churches who were serious about working together to serve their community.

As the meeting ended, the suggestion emerged that the churches represented would form one team to run a Renew space in the Baptist church initially, with a view to rolling out what they learned together across all the buildings with the name 'church' on them in the town. I was delighted. I had dreamed of this happening, but these were early days – this was a key area on the south side of London, offering to share what they had for the sake of the most anxious and isolated.

It is no surprise that God has richly blessed this project. The sense of shared purpose and love is tangible. God loves it when his children play nice!

Give

QUESTIONS

What does the term 'undivided heart' mean to you?

When have you seen real unity in practice?

What problems have you encountered when you have tried to unite with others?

PRAYER

A reflection on lost connection during 2020
Pandemic Pentecost: Connect Again (Matt. 7:12)

How will we connect again?
On what rock will we build?
As rules relax

And loved ones call
How will our days be filled?
What joy for some, for me
To see
My dear missed ones
My family
But, dear Lord
You've shown me those
Who are alone
And have no one to meet
No list of loved ones
In their phone

How will we do for others
What we long for
For our hearts
How will we care like you
Where will we start?

What will we see
When from self-isolated boxes
Church begins to peep
There's kindness, yes
And neighbourly connecting
But oh, such brokenness
And isolation
We have to weep

We need another Pentecost
To birth us into this
To touch a socially distanced world
With heaven's kiss

And flames of fire
That start in every home
To make new spaces
Call them church
Where no one is alone

Our frozen screens
Reveal loves poor reflection
Please Lord, come
Pandemic Pentecost
Across the world
A church unfurled
Restore our weak connection

Resources

In Appendix 1 you will find a menu of agencies, charities, books and resources that a group of us came up with together to help churches engage with wellbeing. This was a united bit of work.

V is for Values

Connect

Whatever one sows, that will he also reap. (Galatians 6:7)

When I am talking to churches about Renew Wellbeing, one of the first things I tell them to do when setting up a centre is to decide together on their values, and display them on the wall. A value denotes what we think is worth our time and attention. A value tells others what is important to us. Values will determine activity. This way the boundaries of what the place is about are clear, and if anyone wants more or doesn't respect those values, it is easier to point at a pre-decided set of family rules than to have many tricky conversations. A shared space could be a 'free for all' with an 'anything goes' attitude and chaos if there were no values.

> Values will determine activity.

We are living with values all the time. But they are often unspoken and we only realize they are there when we go against them in some way. In our homes we have values. You may have spent time in a home where great value is placed on things, on looking after them and keeping them pristine. These are not always the most comfortable of places, even if they are beautiful.

I will talk more about values in Renew spaces because I am coming to believe this task of naming the values is much more vital than I had ever understood, and they are what gives a place sustainable and safe boundaries while making it feel welcoming.

But what timeless truths are there to unpick first about values and God's heart?

Many churches and denominations over the years have tried to express their values as a vison or as a set of religious rules. In doing so they have alienated some, and put people off belonging. I have been part of amazing churches with strong values and yet I am under no illusions that these same churches, with my help and sometimes my leadership, have driven many people away from the God who calls them near.

We can be so keen to make sure people know what our values are, what we don't like, that we sometimes frame those values as rules and negatives.

This realization came when I was unwell with my mental health and came across the Five Ways to Wellbeing.[1] This was at a time when I was struggling with what it meant to be part of any church and not be OK. In most churches, there seemed to be a great value placed on the positive nature of God's goodness as seen in miracles and lives changed. The stories we told from the front of churches would be of healing and provision. Most churches didn't talk much of struggle and doubt and fear, lest we encouraged more of it. If anyone was unwell we would help them, pray for them. The trouble is, when you are mentally unwell there can be a long and drawn-out period of healing needed, not a one-off fix. This didn't sit well within what I was hearing and seeing in churches around me. They were doing a great job of being loving, but for me, the perceived positivity kept me away.

I came across the Five Ways to Wellbeing, five things that people everywhere, not just in the church, need to live with wellbeing, I was struck by how much these five things were what every local church does naturally. Connecting, learning, getting active, taking notice and giving. That's a local church, surely.

The whole Bible is full of these five ways. I can't just pick out one or two verses. Wellbeing runs through the whole book. Strong, clear values of heaven. Value placed on *shalom*.

God's heart is to connect with us. We have seen that. He wants us to connect with each other. We have talked about that too.

Learning from the Word and each other is a strong value. That's why we have so many sermons!

Doing something, serving, having actual practices and habits – getting active – is what we need for faith not to be dead.[2]

Taking notice is another way of describing what happens in prayer and meditation.

Giving ourselves to God in worship, giving our time and our money is a key value for any church.

 Learn

Rereading the book of my important words

My own values are often hidden even from me. I will give time and energy to what I value. Others can see my values before I realize what they are. To help me live more fully in the values that I believe are also Christ's values, I have recorded the most important things God and others have said to me over the years in one book. Every now and again when my mind

247

gets scattered and over-busy, when I forget who and whose I am, I revisit and reread these values.

> I will give time and energy to what I value. Others can see my values before I realize what they are.

I also have a beautiful book made for me by my daughter, when she lived in Africa, out of bits and bobs she found lying around. Every page details a value she has seen lived out in me. I reread it often. By the way, this is a great example of how things can be made new, how beauty can be made from what others consider rubbish. Upcycling that shows us the gospel. If you have ever spent time in Africa, you will know what I mean. If you haven't, check out some of the wonderful clothing made from carrier bags, jewellery made from magazines or footballs made from car tyres.[3]

Both books remind me how God sees me, and what others see; God's Word reminds me, as I read it daily, what he sees and values. To rehearse the truth and essence of these values at least every month is really helpful when I tend to take on the values of others or the world around me.

When we first started renew37, we knew that we needed to display our values on the wall so that we could just point at them to remind people what sort of place this was. I found a ready-made arty wooden thing at a garden centre with family values like 'speak kindly' etc. on it. We crossed out a few inappropriate ones that involved always smiling and hugging and popped it on the wall. It sort of did the trick.

But I have learned so much as the movement has progressed; many of our teams have been so thoughtful in the way they have set up their values statement to make it welcoming and positive but setting clear boundaries to make it clear how the place was to be treated.

These are the value statements that greet you on a lovely, colourful pull-up banner when you enter Renew Well in the Isle of Man.[4]

Our Values
Each person is unique
YOU are unique and precious.
We want this to be a space where we can each both give and receive. If you have a hobby, an idea, a **welcoming** word for someone, please share it.

A respectful and quiet space
Let's make this a judgement-free zone where everyone feels welcome and accepted.

WE ask that there be:
No selling, no heated politics, no 'fixing' people, and no proselytising.

 Get Active

I asked our friends at Sanctuary Ministries UK[5] about what values they felt were key for a church serious about becoming mental health-friendly, and a safe place. This is what the CEO Corin Pilling said:

A great starting place to consider values when it comes to mental health – or any element of our life together – is through the lens of the kingdom of God. If we aspire to be offering a true welcome, are we aware and informed as a community? Are we equipped to offer appropriate support? These are foundational questions for us as we seek to be a community where all can feel at home – a place of sanctuary.

Yet there's also another kingdom value we should consider: participation. God calls us to be co-creators in building his kingdom. In the kingdom, even the most difficult life experiences and circumstances qualify us with a unique gift to offer, and we're invited to bring what we can. Engaging in this question moves mental health beyond a pastoral issue.

The next stage of the journey is this: Are we removing the barriers to participation? Or, are we unconsciously disqualifying those who face difficulty? Are the voices and gifts of those of us who live with difficulties starting to shape who we are as a community? If we take this value seriously, we'll see communities which reflect the breadth of the kingdom. It's not for the faint-hearted, it might be at times messy and complicated – but it's a vital stage of the journey.

 Take Notice

The values of Renew Wellbeing are written down. But I am much more interested in what they are beginning to look like at a national level and how they are infiltrating every area of church and community.

Being prayerful looks like quiet spaces being prayed in up and down the country. It looks like people observing still moments of prayer alone and together all over the place. It looks like me actually praying before I do anything else each day, pausing whenever I hold a cuppa, breathing in his presence. Being prayerful looks like turning up each day on a Zoom screen with others from around the UK to simply go through morning prayer together. I love those moments.

To be prayerful is not just a value in my head or heart; being prayerful looks like something in practice in this charity.

Being present is not just a key value, it looks like others giving up time to join me daily on a Zoom screen. It looks like hundreds of folk spending time each week in Renew spaces, just showing up even if no visitors come. It looks like people choosing to really listen to each other, to wait for each other, to be kind to each other with no agenda. It looks like me sitting down, not running round trying to fix everyone. It looks like stillness and quiet sometimes. It can even look like time-wasting.

Being in partnership means as a charity spending time honouring and talking with other mental health charities, making sure we share resources and hold each other up. It looks like putting aside time to attend meetings with mental health professionals, even when nothing comes of it. It means looking out for partners who are already doing what we dream of and getting alongside them. It means sharing good news and bad within the Renew family so we can learn from each other.

Our values look like something in practice. They lead to practices, habits, a way of being.

Give

QUESTIONS

What would you say your top three personal values are?

What values would you love to see in action in your community?

Do you think it matters whether you let people know what your values are or not in community projects like Renew centres?

PRAYER

A blessing for vulnerable values (Num. 6:24–26; Matt. 6:10)

May he who truly loves you bless you
To know that
It's OK

Not to be OK
In fact
It's the only way
To open
Hands
And doors and plans
To see the new within the old
That there's more blessing
Than our churchy little boxes can hold

May the Lord keep you, keep you
In tension
Of lament and praise, keep you
Not knowing how many days we have
Keep you outside
Your careful

Church-based plan
Keep you applauding in your streets
For your fellow man

May the Lord make his face shine on you
And may it shine right
Through you
And may the things that you thought were you get caught
    up in the blaze

Of his shining face

And may he give you peace, not happy moments for the
few who made it to the Meetings who
Already knew
His peace
But deep *shalom*
That joins the many
But seeks the one
Who cries alone

Peace
Shalom
Wellbeing
Spoken
Blessing given … his kingdom come on earth

As it is in heaven

Resources

For excellent resources for your church journey to becoming a sanctuary for all: http://www.sanctuarymental
health.org/uk

For values banners and statements for a Renew space:
www.renewwellbeing.org.uk resources page

$\boxed{\text{W}}$ is for Wait

 **Connect**

Be still before the LORD and wait patiently for him . . . (Psalm 37:7)

I was tempted to make this 'W is for wellbeing'. But the whole book is an attempt to discover the depth of the word 'wellbeing' and the invitation is for you to explore it and find what wellbeing means to you. So instead I take the word 'wait' here.

Waiting is not something that comes naturally to me. I try to choose the shortest queue in the shop, would prefer to take a long route to somewhere rather than be in a traffic jam, often don't make the best coffee, as you are supposed to give the boiled water a minute or so before pouring (so I'm told) and I just can't wait. Christmas usually sees me peeking in the corners of presents, and deciding we can open the chocolates way before Christmas day. Waiting – not a strong point. I think there will be others who agree.

In Isaiah 40:31, as we have seen in 'R is for renew', it talks about us being renewed as we wait. All we have to do is wait.

I love this prophetic image; the way we are to be renewed is simply to wait. The Hebrew word here for 'wait' is also a fascination of mine. The word is *qavah*, which is active waiting. It is the same word used of a spider making a web. The idea is that we can actively spin gossamer threads through our habits and practices as we wait for God, and in doing so will be all the more ready to receive, to catch, his goodness.

The waiting is all we are required to do and this describes for me what it feels like to engage in wellbeing habits like prayer and hobbies and meditation. I am not making wellbeing happen, I am waiting to catch wellbeing which only God can make happen. But the active waiting makes me more ready to do that. This is not simply moaning and sighing and complaining about my lack. It is believing goodness will come along again and preparing to catch it.

There is also talk of God waiting in the Bible. In Isaiah 30 God says he 'waits' for us (Isa. 30:18). The Hebrew word here is *chakah*. This comes from a word that implies long-term tarrying. It is also used of processes that make a long-term impression, like piercing or carving. There is a sense here that God's waiting is productive and extremely patient, and no one comes out the other end of it the way they came in. To wait seems so passive, such a waste of time. It seems disrespectful to keep God waiting or to imply that God needs us to do something before he can act. But the Hebrew is clear, *chakah*. To wait. Here we have a God who is longing for us, 'the LORD waits to be gracious to you' (Isa. 30:18).

This is a God who shows us love when we are 'still sinners' (Rom. 5:8). He does take the initiative, for which I am so glad. But I do find it rather wonderful that this is also a God who waits for the right time to step towards us. He doesn't force us to love him, or come to him.

In the story of the prodigal son in Luke 15, we see a father waiting for his son to come to his senses and return home. We then see the father running to meet him. But he does a lot of looking and waiting. This is said to be a picture of how God sees us, loves us, and waits for us. He will meet us more than half way when we come back to him, but he won't force us. But

I have to weigh this image against the story of the lost sheep in Matthew 8:12,13, where the shepherd does not wait but goes out looking. It seems there are no hard and fast rules. God treats us all as we need to be treated. He is prepared to wait; if he thinks you need time to be ready, he will wait.

This has been and continues to be a source of great wonder to me. A God who is in no hurry. Who will wait. It has formed the practices of my heart and of Renew Wellbeing.

 Learn

Web-weaving to catch the goodness

When I was unwell, I have to be honest and say I really did not wait like this. I was not patient. I did not remember there was a God who would wait for me. I was convinced it was the end of me. I was fairly sure God had abandoned me. It was my lovely husband and his steady, unworried belief that one day all would be well again that kept the web ready in those dark days. It was my children and their love for me, still seeing me as they always had, that kept me ready to receive goodness again. It was the prayers of my friends holding their metaphorical shields around me while I lay in bed that meant I didn't give up. Sometimes we need a bit of help with all this active waiting.

I am learning each day that waiting is a part of being human. It means I don't need to over-medicalize when I am feeling low. I can choose to wait. I don't mean to say that you should wait if you know you are really struggling, but for me, the panic that I have a massive problem and I need to act straight away or it will all get worse subsides when I begin to grasp this word 'wait' as a key word for my wellbeing.

Once I grasp that God is not absent, he is active in the waiting time, he is carving something, he is present in the space and waiting for me, I can settle much better into whatever season I need to be in.

> I am learning each day that waiting is a part of being human.

When I begin to grasp that I can actively wait and spin that web of habits and hobbies and creativity, and that the feelings will change one day, I begin to get less anxious about how long everything takes. Time becomes a gift to be embraced if I remember that waiting is not a bad thing.

What I have sometimes discovered is that I am not waiting 'for' something, but that the waiting itself is the thing. It is a bit like when you do strength-based exercise (or so I am told!). In the still position of a plank, the muscles are active and strengthening. It is not so much a position to get you to the next place, but the waiting is the best position in which to strengthen your inner muscles.

God's *chavah* meets my *qavah*. He carves and I spin and when we meet again I am ready for his love in a new way. The year of darkness and emptiness was not a wasted year. As I look back, God was actively waiting and, I suppose, so was I.

 **Get Active**

Here is Jo from Northallerton Renew talking about how much waiting they had to do to be able to work together on their amazing project at the Living Rooms.

Five churches in Northallerton were already working together on a few projects and had identified that mental wellbeing and social isolation were the greatest needs in our community. A vision to set up a community hub was at the talking stage when Ruth came to speak at a ladies day in November 2016 and this provided the catalyst for the Living Rooms. From that day we had a team joining with the steering group who wanted to make a Renew space happen. We started praying and fundraising.

One of the team started making contacts with NHS and North Yorkshire County Council mental health teams and other local voluntary agencies. We applied for charitable status so that the denominations had joint ownership from the start. This application process took time and there were many delays, which was incredibly frustrating.

Simultaneously, we were looking for town centre premises at an affordable rent and this too took time. Properties were either dilapidated, too big, too small, or had unaffordable rents. Eventually we negotiated the lease on an old flooring shop in an arcade just off the high street with office spaces above. With the financial help of all five churches and some grant funding from the councils and the Police and Crime Commissioner, we refurbished the premises upstairs and down.

. . . There was a lot of waiting and planning and meetings and preparing but looking back, there was a lot of 'holding' and 'growing' in that time.

It took time to find a way to work together well, but there is such blessing in the unity we have now between our churches and it is much better than if the largest church had taken the lead and set it up on behalf of us all. There was such a meeting of minds as we planned the interior design of the premises, and support from local businesses was generous. We held an event in the local community centre with a pop-up Renew space – 250 people attended. We grew a volunteer team from the churches and the community. We made friends with neighbouring businesses in the Arcade. Momentum grew!

By the time we opened in November 2019 it was 'full-on' and busy, and quite soon we had the challenge of how to ensure 'a quiet shared space'!

 Take Notice

Sarah, who heads up the thinking around Renew spaces for youth and children, as well as being East of England coordinator, knows a bit about waiting. She writes:

In January 2020 I began to work with Renew Wellbeing to develop the idea for children, young people and families. I was excited to set up a pilot project with a local school where I had a contact on the staff, and the youth worker at a church that already had a Renew space was up for having a go. I began talking to the school and they were keen, so I set up a meeting with the head teacher to get the go-ahead. We arranged that for 23 March . . . The meeting got cancelled, as did every other meeting. Everyone had bigger things to deal with and the Children, Youth and Families (CYF) project went to the bottom of the list. We all knew that children and young people would need support more than ever, but everyone was focusing on the basics and starting something new was a step too far. I carried on thinking and praying and trying to work out how to help churches start something for young people when nobody had any spare capacity to have a go, and young people were absolutely not keen to meet on Zoom for something they didn't understand.

The past year has been a time of waiting. All through that time I've been hoping that the time was right, and someone would be able to have a go, but as Lockdowns two and three followed, and I have had my own struggles and challenges dealing with COVID, it's only now that I'm able to start writing resources. At times I felt like I was waiting for God to make the circumstances right. I kept telling myself that he knew from the beginning what was coming so I need to trust him in the waiting and dreaming; when the time was right, I would know. That was hard at times – there was a sense of failure, and isolation; my patience wore thin at times, with myself and the circumstances. But what I have also realized is that he was waiting for me. He had plans for Renew for children, young people and families, and those plans included me. But he was willing to wait for me to be ready for action as well. As I've worked with churches setting up Renew spaces over the past year with my role as coordinator for the East of England, and listened to their stories, it's been clear that just as we wait on the Lord, he waits for us to be up for following where he wants to lead.

Give

QUESTIONS

What is the longest time you have had to wait for something? How did it feel?

What helps you when you have to wait?

What does 'wait for the LORD'[1] mean to you?

PRAYER

Wait
For the Lord
But Lord, this is so hard
You do not know
How much I long
To see it happen straight away

Oh yes, I know
How hard it is to wait
I hear you say
I've waited
Am still waiting
For you to
Slow down
Show up
And pray
To come to me
To stay
Wait for me
As I wait for you
And I will take the weight
On me
And in this waiting room
You'll be set free
From every weight
While you wait

Resources

John Mark Comer, *The Ruthless Elimination of Hurry*. This is a wonderful book encouraging slow, steady habits and exploring what sabbath looks like.

$\boxed{X}$ Marks the Spot

 **Connect**

We have this treasure in jars of clay . . . (2 Corinthians 4:7)

So I have cheated! I know you have been wondering as you approach the X, how I was going to spiritualize an X-ray, or was I going to go with the Greek word '*xenos*' meaning stranger and wax lyrical about how bad xenophobia is for anyone's wellbeing. I could have done that, but the simple letter itself is enough to remind me of all those years as a primary school teacher doing amazing topics. My favourite was a treasure island-type of topic and making treasure maps and marking the treasure with an X. This is what I think of every time I see an X, not a kiss or that I have something wrong, or even multiplication. No, the way my mind works when I see an X is, there must be treasure. An X was used to mark a place so that it could be found again. So X is for 'X marks the spot'. I want to talk about treasure.

As we near the end of my alphabet I am delighted to be able to explore this weird concept. Wellbeing, as we have discovered in these pages, means so many things to so many different people. It is simple, yet rich and varied. It is hard to define, yet we know when we have found it.

As I explore X I want to drop a few markers in places where I have found wellbeing. Wellbeing for me is found in my relationship with God, so a chapter devoted to places may seem a bit odd!

The Bible refers to us as God's 'dwelling place' (Eph. 2:22); he places his treasure in us. It also speaks of our hearts being where our treasure is (Matt. 6:21). There are stories about buried treasure told by Jesus. So I wanted to mark where I have found treasure in my trek through wellbeing words.

The Bible is rich with treasure. This is my first 'place' to put an X. This book that I look at every day, or most days, of my life is a veritable goldmine. God speaks through it to me. I particularly mark a big X in the middle of the book in the Psalms and a big X in the Gospels. I encourage you to have a daily habit with both psalms and Gospels if you don't have one already. I have found such richness in these pages. I never get to the bottom of the treasure chest.

There is so much to be learned about wellbeing from so many sources, but if you have never read the Bible I would say you are missing the greatest handbook for wellbeing ever written. From the first words of the 'In the beginning'[1] God to the fantastic descriptions of the river of life in Revelation 22 at the end of the book, there is a vision of wellbeing. Yes, there is much that is difficult to understand, but the Bible spans years and years of history and many styles of writing. The God of wellbeing has marked treasure there for us to find. His love, his grace are woven through the whole story.

> If you have never read the Bible I would say you are missing the greatest handbook for wellbeing ever written.

Then we see the most unbelievable treasure as Jesus chooses the cross to show his love for us. Here is a great mystery. God himself taking my place, winning life for me. X marks the spot where all of life converges in a single moment in history. I am captivated by the cross.

Connecting with this cross connects us to the whole of life, I believe, and in this connection wellbeing begins to take a whole different meaning.

 Learn

Learning to map the treasure spots

I am learning to mark places and times, and review what I am beginning to understand. For this I use a journal. The practice of journaling has been a strong habit for me for many years; I have loads of notebooks full of words. I use them to chat to God, to work out what I am thinking. But it is only recently I have realized that treasure is contained in these pages, and I now take time at the end of each year to review the year that has gone and read through my journals to spot where God has shown up, and where the learning about wellbeing has been happening. I then write a psalm to the year that has gone and one for the year to come.

The change came for me when I was unwell that long, dark year. Up until then I would have said my notebooks were full of rubbish and that my words had no value. I would have insisted that someone burnt them if anything were to happen to me, not because they were full of secrets but because I would be embarrassed for anyone to see how up and down I was. I still am. The difference now is that I don't think anyone's thoughts are rubbish, so I try not to level that accusation at myself. What

I recognize I am thinking and feeling just is. My journals are an attempt to live honestly and authentically in my skin.

I have begun to look out for treasure and turn a corner of a page or mark with a highlighter anything that seems to be of value that I have learned the hard way. The philosopher Søren Kierkegaard once said, 'We live our lives forward but we only understand them backwards.'[2] My journaling is an attempt not to miss the treasure you can only see with hindsight.

I also mark actual pictures and verses and promises in a special notebook called 'words of my life'. These are significant things people have said to me and prayed for me, words from the Bible people have given to me over the years that I wanted to treasure and not forget. I go to this book often, when I am feeling low or confused, and remind myself that what God has said is still true.

I mark places too. Before we set up renew37 I didn't think I really believed places could be sacred. I thought it was only people that carried the presence of God. But I am now convinced that some places, due to the prayer that has been in them, are full of wellbeing and I mark these spots.

One is very close to home. A chair in the corner of our front room looking out over the garden is my prayer chair. I sit here with my cup each day and God meets me there. Another is on my daily walk by the canal with the dog. There is a beautiful willow tree where I always sense the beauty of the Creator. When I was unwell there was a certain bench in a country park near us that felt like a secret place between me and God. My wellbeing bench.

There are other places, harder to access like Fflad-y-Brenin[3] in Pembrokeshire or the Mother House of the Northumbria Community.[4] There is the beauty of Scargill House in Yorkshire and the welcome of St Joseph Prayer Centre in Formby.[5] There is my friend's little beach chalet in Dunster and the beautiful island where I was born, the Isle of Man. There are places where it feels like God is nearer. He isn't, I'm sure of it. Otherwise I am moving! He is as near to me in a shopping centre and the traffic jam, but it may be that I can hear better in the beauty of certain places.

The discovery that places could bring wellbeing was what led to the opening of renew37. I write more about the frustration that led to this in *Slow Down, Show Up and Pray* in a section called 'The 500-mile big think'.[6] This refers to driving back from a visit to a retreat centre and being really irritated that those who needed places of peace most would never access some of the most beautiful spaces only the few could find or afford. It made me want to have a place in every town and village for anyone to find wellbeing. I want an X to mark every street.

 **Get Active**

One of our wonderful hosts in Chipping Campden started a Renew centre after hearing God speak as they prayer-walked. This was a regular thing for her. It is a great habit to walk and pray and listen to God, and it enables you to see what he sees in your community.

Tooty says this:

Betty and I do have one special spot where, during our weekly walk around the town, we both truly felt the presence of God

. . . as for some time we'd been praying for guidance on what we could/should be doing . . .

We were walking a field which runs along the back of Campden . . . we sat and rested on a large fallen tree trunk, gnarled and weathered . . . it was so, so quiet and still all around us, amid the thistles and sheep droppings, sheep peacefully grazing – we truly both felt the presence and voice of God telling us to press on with Renew . . .

The same day we collected some smaller gnarled branches and fashioned the small cross which we use in our quiet space.

During the pandemic lockdown these wonderful women did not feel able to manage the technology to keep their space running so they did what they knew how to do. They walked and prayed and dropped off gifts as they went.

When we've delivered gifts during COVID it's been a case of making a silent prayer as we push the package through the letter box, then subsequently we are able to chat when the recipients (mostly) phone to say thank you.

 Take Notice

Sometimes places where God is at work are harder to spot. When I was leading New Life Baptist Church, we were looking for a space for a permanent home as a church. We had met in school halls for years and many felt it was time to get a building. I have never been that sure about buildings, as I have seen them tie people down and have seen many begin to believe the building is the church. However, I am realizing how helpful a place can be now.

The journey to find a place for New Life Baptist Church to meet was long and convoluted. I looked at nearly every empty space in our area with shiny faith-filled eyes only to be disappointed over and over again. This was an expensive part of town and there were already fourteen church buildings. It felt to me that we needed to think outside the box and go somewhere a bit different. There were years of praying and searching and leading people up dead-ends.

At one point we were in discussions to acquire a massive, rambling, stately home of a place in the centre of town. It would have eaten all our resources and then some. At other points an entire block of flats, a pub, a warehouse by the river: each seemed like it held some promise, each took time and energy and led nowhere.

We continued to meet in a school and a community centre and our homes. We were still church.

Then one day as I was sitting meeting with a few folk in my local café, Tiffin Tea House, with the most excellent Battenberg cake, I was approached by the owners who knew me well by this time due to the many cake-filled meetings.

They were planning to take a lease on the property next door to increase capacity and asked if the church would like to share the use and the rent.

This was a tiny property. It had been an office of some sort. As a café space it would hold twenty to thirty people. This was not the stately home, the pub, the warehouse we had imagined. This was not the place to gather as church on Sundays, but to be church during the week. It challenged our ideas of what sort of building we needed to be church in. But we immediately knew God's hand was in this. X marked the spot.

The process from then on was by no means straightforward. The church was amazing and voted unanimously to go for something which was nothing like what they wanted. They spotted God's hand at work. They saw the X that marked the treasure and put all their treasure with his. This would mean still hiring halls for Sundays. This would not be their dream but it might be God's dream, so they went for it.

From the January of the conversation it was six long months until the keys were finally handed over and we could get started preparing the space to be renew37.

This was a place where treasure lay. The treasure of changed lives and belonging for the isolated. A place to be. A place to pray. A place to dare and imagine and connect.

X marks this spot. There is treasure here.

Give

QUESTIONS

Do you have a place where it is easier for you to sense God's presence?

Do you have a place where community meets that fills you with wellbeing?

In what ways has God spoken to you through the Bible? Where is the treasure for you?

PRAYER

'Where your treasure is . . .' (Matt. 6:21)

Where is my treasure?
Not in buried chests
In old forgotten haunts
Deep in the past

Not in bank accounts
Here in the present
That don't last
Not in dreams and hopes
Way off in the future that dies
But right here
In the present
My treasure lies
Giving myself to you
I find you are my treasure
True
My treasure true of joy and peace
Deposit account of deep love
Current account
Of kindness released
This is where
I bank my heart
This is where I start
To save
Become the giver
Treasure found
In the One that gave

Resources

Charlie Mackesy, *The Boy, the Mole, the Fox and the Horse*.
A treasure of a book for your soul whatever your age.

Y is for You

 **Connect**

I have loved you with an everlasting love . . . (Jeremiah 31:3)

So we near the end of the alphabet; this is where it gets personal. Throughout this wellbeing alphabet I have been circling round several very simple truths that hold me in my wellbeing adventure. This is relational for me. We do not live in a vacuum; our wellbeing affects everyone. I also believe it is a matter of identity. So the letter Y is for You.

Firstly the *you* I am referring to with this letter is God himself. He is the one and only 'other' whom we all need. We can know him and therefore we can know ourselves.

Secondly, the *you* I am talking about is myself. This is personal.

Thirdly, the *you* I refer to is you. Yes, you. Every person ever made. Every person who ever had breath and a pulse affects my wellbeing; we all need each other. Nothing is ever just personal. Wellbeing looks like something when it is shared. It looks like God's love.

Connecting with God is the beginning of this for me. Connecting with him first enables me to connect with myself and others. The identity crisis that leads to poor mental health, that led me to a mental health crisis, starts and ends right here. It's all about you. Me. But mostly it's all about him.

Identity is an interesting thing. We all think we know who we are, but so much of what I was thinking about myself was what others had told me and spoken over me. So much of my identity was around the lies I was telling myself in my worried head. Even during the good days my identity was in a sort of crisis, because I thought a good day happened because of something I had got right that day, someone I had helped.

> Identity that leads to wellbeing is grounded in how loved and accepted we are … my identity crisis was not about me but about who I thought God was.

To live with our identity caught up in doing, not just being, led me to breakdown. I wonder what your identity crisis looks like? Because I think we are all having one, at least some days.

Identity that leads to wellbeing is grounded in how loved and accepted we are, so I am beginning to realize my identity crisis was not about me but about who I thought God was.

Somewhere in my Christian upbringing I had formed a vison of a God who needed to be pleased with me to 'use' me. I refer to this as 'spatula theology' in my previous book. I don't quite know where I got this from. I was surrounded with loving, hard-working Christian folk, but somehow I believed that God was a little disappointed with me and much more pleased with those who stood on the platform, had the perfect praying families and wrote the Christian books (oh, irony of ironies).

I now realize there are no such things as celebrity Christians and perfect families. There are certainly no such things as people who know all the answers and write them in books! There are only humans, broken sinful humans, with stories of grace and forgiveness. Loved and accepted people. The only labels I need.

I now am beginning to see how very good and trustworthy and kind God is. I am rereading the harsher passages in the Old Testament and looking for the face of Jesus who came to show us what God is like. We get to read the Bible backwards and know that he is all love, and if we are to understand anything else we might need to take another look.

I am learning to trust the hands around the cup. The hands of a God who is so far beyond my understanding, yet who is so in love with me that my identity is wrapped up more and more in what he thinks about me.

 Learn

Learning that I am the project

I can accept that this is all about God. I can even cope with it all being about other people, but I struggle daily to believe that God loves me, really loves me, as I am. I am the wellbeing project. I am learning to embrace this and live out my own wellbeing language and habits by practising the simple things I have talked about in this book. Holding the cup, I feel his love for me. His hands; my life held. Reading the Scriptures, praying the Psalms, I repeat daily who God is to my soul in case I have redesigned him in my own image or in the shape of the events around me. I choose each day to speak the truth of God's character over myself because that is where my own identity comes from.

At the end of prayer each morning when we speak the words from Psalm 103:4 over each other, over ourselves, I choose to believe I am loved and that he 'crowns' me 'with compassion'.[1] I choose to sit and receive that love and let that define me. I don't always succeed. But as sure as my teeth will not be healthy if I don't brush them each day, my soul will not have wellbeing if I don't remind myself of the most important thing about myself each day. I will spend all day looking for love and acceptance if I don't realize I am already loved.

> God won't love me more or less, dependent on what I do or say.

I am not saying this is a legalistic habit that attracts God's love like a superstitious need in me to keep God close. No, he is already close. He won't love me more or less, dependent on what I do or say. It is for me that I need to carry out these habits and make these choices. It is because I am beginning to think I am worth it. That my soul deserves the time as much as my teeth.

Learning who I am is a lifetime's journey and is so tied up with learning who God is that the best practice for me of self-compassion is not to look at myself, but to look at him and see myself reflected in his eyes of love.

 Get Active

Getting active with the letter Y takes me to the fact that my wellbeing affects the wellbeing of others, of you, and vice versa. It would be impossible to overstate what a huge privilege this adventure with Renew Wellbeing has been for me personally. The people I have met and am meeting along the way are wonderful. There is such a wide variety of gifting and character, but such a similar heart among those I am meeting to see wellbeing renewed, to be more transparent, more present. It is delightful to have conversation after conversation with people who have all had a similar dream of a place where all can be equal, all can find a place to belong. It is truly humbling and very enriching.

Not least has been the great team I work with now, most of whom came to me without me even looking and during a global pandemic when team growth was not a thing happening in other organizations.

Some have been with me, loyally choosing to take the same winding path with me, for years. This never ceases to amaze me, that God puts a few people in your life who will stick with you through thick and thin. What a gift to have people who know you well and love you anyway.

Then there have been people I have known for years and our paths have gone separate ways and God has converged them again. People with amazing gifts that complement my own. People who know me well enough to speak their minds.

There have been those who I met randomly at conferences or even in motorway services who have gone on to be lifelong friends and indispensable team members.

There are those who have been recommended to me by others who knew exactly what I needed and were thoughtful enough to make connections.

There are those who God had been preparing for ministry and who were already out on a limb, unsure of what the future held but keeping on saying yes to him until they found someone articulating exactly what they dreamed of.

There are those who were leading church faithfully and already sensing the call to something new and different, who could lead from within local church.

There were those who God sent to walk the path of wellbeing with us for a season to prepare them for something more and different, who brought unique gifts to the table and shared them willingly and generously before moving on, taking the Renew family in their heart with them.

What has astounded me is that despite all coming from different backgrounds, church settings, and geographical locations, we are so united in our desire to see wellbeing renewed. Despite, at the time of writing, not having been physically in the same room due to COVID-19 – even though we have worked as a team for a year – we would consider each other to be deephearted friends, and our weekly meetings and catch-ups bring life and energy to each of us.

The family of God is already remarkable. So diverse and yet together as one, displaying the character of God in all its creativity and beauty. I suppose what I am saying is that if you add in the brokenness of mental ill health, a few shared habits, a desire to see wellbeing renewed, a willingness to slow down and the need to learn to pray, the bond increases and the variety is all the more precious.

You, dear friend reading this, are part of this rich picture he is painting.

 Take Notice

From around the UK, our coordinators share some of that uniqueness as they have seen it in the Renew spaces in their patch. This is the amazing treasure that is you, the other, in whom I see the beauty of God. Here are some reflections from our Renew Wellbeing team around the UK.

Fiona, who oversees the North of England, says this:

I just love my northern Renew spaces and am in awe of their determination to keep on being prayerful and present during the pandemic. Here are a few examples:

Renew 233 in Burnley spent several months in prayerful preparation as a host team before opening in person in late 2020. They have consistently stayed open in person (permitted as a support group) for a small number of regulars who cannot meet online, and have persevered through a difficult winter with their Renew space every Friday afternoon. I have seen such blessing to both regulars and hosts through this time.

Renew Wellbeing Lumb in Rossendale have a special place in my heart as this is my own church family. They have met on Zoom since January 2021 and as the lockdown eased they started meeting outside – this is no mean feat in the hills of Lancashire; woolly hats are essential! Their speciality is that they have reached out to the isolated in their own worshipping community first, and have created a group of hosts and regulars who are looking forward to extending their welcome to the wider community.

Renew Wellbeing Eden in Appleby-in-Westmorland are amazing. Having met for several months on Zoom, they are planning as a group of local churches from different denominations to open up Renew spaces in several rural locations across the area. Wellbeing will indeed be renewed in Cumbria.

Renew 5 in Northallerton have inspired me as they have found ways to be present, indoors, outdoors and online throughout the pandemic. Their host group has many hosts who have shielded; these hosts have met online through this period to pray for Renew and their regulars. Surely this demonstrates true commitment to being present, prayerful and in partnership.

Coordinator Margaret says this about her centres in the West of England:

I love to see the faithfulness of groups like Renew 55, finding ways to stay connected to their regulars who can't use technology, the enthusiasm of groups like Renew Nailsworth who are continually planning creative ways to reopen, or Renew Devizes who are enthusing other groups to plan and open Renew spaces; Renew Nailsea who have maintained a presence throughout lockdown, using technology and open spaces as well as their building, and Renew Chew and Yeo Valley who are exploring opening Renew spaces to reconnect with village communities across the valley. There are many other stories I could mention, every single West Renew Wellbeing space has an amazing and unique story to tell of how God is renewing wellbeing in their context.

Ben, our coordinator for the South, says:

Renew 23 in Purley is a vibrant yet deeply peaceful community. The hosts and regulars alike have created a culture that is truly life-giving, and you leave the space feeling a real sense of refreshment. They are also very creative, having thrown themselves into ideas such as Outdoors Renew.

Renew 11 in Canterbury is a relatively new addition to the family, and they are full of exciting ideas about how their Renew space may serve the nearby community. In particular, this outward-looking perspective is inspiring thoughts around engaging with youth and students, and various other groups.

Sarah, who coordinates the Eastern part of England, has so many centres to choose from. As this was the area where Renew started, there are many amazing examples of God at work. She tells us here about the one she established. She has a fantastic partnership with the local council in Leicestershire and was invited to County Hall several times to speak to leaders there.

I set up Renew 67 in the church café in spring 2017. A faithful team of volunteers meant that the group met every week, and we quickly got known around the area as a safe space. When lockdown happened, regulars couldn't do Zoom so 'met' in WhatsApp in the usual timeslot. I have since moved on and Wendy took over leading – they are still keeping in touch and beginning to meet in real life again. It's a brilliant example of how even a small church can still do something that supports the anxious, the lonely and those in need of some company.

Naomi works with the South Wales Baptist Association to plant Renew centres in South Wales. She is loving the new interest, and there are lots of green shoots at the time of writing. She says this about the centre she established in Cardiff:

The atmosphere at Renew @ The Ark really encapsulates a sense of *shalom*. It is a precious haven amongst the busyness of life. It offers a place of peace and prayer that helps promote wellbeing in a way that's genuine and authentic; I think that's what makes it attractive and welcoming to people. One of our regular attenders says, 'I have found a space where I am "at home" and safe to be me. I have discovered a hobby I love which takes me out of my head, and I have found a wonderful, supportive bunch of friends.'

In Scotland there are so many centres joining us as I write that I am coming to terms with the fact that this is God's work, not mine! A control freak in recovery, I am learning to trust God and see him cultivate this garden of centres.

In the Isle of Man there are several Renew spaces. These were the vision and dream of Alison, who was a wonderful pioneer and charity leader with a massive heart for her community and who started the first Manx Renew space. Alison sadly died way too soon. But the seeds she planted and the vision she had is alive and well. Renew Well in Douglas is a lovely space, full of light and life, next door to Broadway Baptist Church, and Renew Slaynt-as-Shee[2] in Peel run by a lovely team from the Methodist church are testaments to Alison's compassion for people and determination for each person to know how loved they are. It is a joy to see Renew spaces begin to flourish on the island where I was born and raised.

Northern Ireland is just opening up as I write and a group of churches on the north coast are planning a Renew space. One of the team said simply, 'I wish we'd had something like this years ago when I was so lonely!'

Each person is so precious. Each space is so unique.

He is the author of wellbeing and he has written you in to his story of wellbeing.

Give

QUESTIONS

Who is God to you? What images, words and descriptions come to mind? What aspects of his character have you misunderstood?

How would you describe yourself? What are your greatest strengths and gifts?

Which people have influenced your life and encouraged you, and how? Maybe take a moment to thank them if you can.

PRAYER

It's personal
This life
He died to give

It's personal
This hope
That took his breath
It's personal
This joy that seeps through pain
This breakfast-cooking risen Lord
Who came
He's personal
And the person
It's you
It's me
Out of the darkness.
Spacious place
He sets us free
And it's every other person
That ever breathed
Or laughed, or cried
For every single precious one that's died
It's personal

Resources

Gerard Kelly, *Spoken Worship*. A beautiful collection of poems by a good friend who has influenced my life.

Z zz . . .

 **Connect**

I . . . lie down and sleep in peace . . . (Psalm 4:8, NRSV)

So again I am going to cheat. Although zebras, zips and zoos are all good, I want to end this alphabet with the letter Z representing sleep. You know, the zzz that cartoons use when a character is sleeping, to show the snores? I hope you do, or this last letter will confuse you! I feel it is vital to end this exploration of wellbeing by saying it is not the end. Just as sleep restores us and we start all over again the next day, wellbeing is a daily thing. We will sleep and then wake, and the quest for lives full of wellbeing continues.

This is an invitation to language-learning and lifestyle habits, and to work out your own A–Z of wellbeing.

This could be an A–Z that helps connect us in common language, or it may at least provide a starting point for each of us to become more fluent in the language of being human.

So zzz represents the fact that I will sleep and wake again and learn some more.

In the Bible, sleep is seen as a gift from God. God is with us as we sleep. There are references to sleeping soundly because he watches over us. It also suggests that God doesn't sleep; he is ever vigilant.[1]

I love the way God speaks to people in their sleep when the normal filters are turned off. Dreams like Jacob's ladder,[2] Joseph's instruction to flee with the baby Jesus and Mary for safety,[3] Peter's dream on a rooftop,[4] have all led me to take notice of dreams where God seems to be speaking. I ask him to speak in my dreams and be with me in my sleep. A couple of the most profound and life-changing words from God have come while I was asleep. Conversely, I have the weirdest dreams I would not like to read anything into at all, usually involving toilets and department stores.

I know God is still with me in my sleep. I have had whole seasons of my life where sleep just wouldn't come and it can feel like a form of torture. We all need sleep to recover and be restored.

One of the key passages that informs our charity is a little story Jesus tells in Mark 4. This is the story of a farmer who plants seeds and then it says, 'He sleeps and rises night and day, and the seed sprouts and grows; he knows not how' (v. 27). I have loved reflecting on this important little story over the years I have watched Renew Wellbeing grow from one centre to fifty centres to potentially 200 centres at the time of writing. I genuinely 'know not how' this little seed of an idea that I needed for my wellbeing has grown. God does all the hard work, that's for sure. It seems my role is the waking and the sleeping bit; I interpret this as my need to simply be true to the rhythms of wellbeing as I understand them, to keep on keeping on with the wellbeing language-learning. To wake and to sleep. He brings the growth.

This leads me to include these zzzs in my alphabet as they represent the fact that as mere humans, even when we sleep, life carries on. We can rest. There is a God. It isn't me. What a relief!

> We can rest. There is a God. It isn't me. What a relief!

Learn

Rewinding to unwind

I am not going to talk here about learning to sleep. I'm not that good at it. I have learned to offload to God before sleep using the prayer of Examen, and it usually slows down my anxious thoughts and helps me sleep more peacefully. But not always. There are seasons in life when sleep is more difficult, and I don't want to make anyone feel that because they aren't sleeping well they won't have good wellbeing. It helps to sleep well, but for those with small children, or time of life sleep problems, there is still hope. He is with you through the 'watches of the night' (Ps. 63:6).

I am learning about rhythm, though, and to let a day go and accept the gift of the next one. That is what I want to end with, with these zzzs. The end of an alphabet. The end of a day. The possibility of a new day. This waking and sleeping rhythm reflects the wellbeing patterns that I am beginning to embrace, to learn to work with, not fight against.

But I have also learned or am learning a lot about wellbeing from working with those facing their final sleep. It may seem a bit depressing to end a book about wellbeing by talking about death, but it is one of the certain things any of us will face, unless the Lord returns first.

To face it without fear, with peace, is the ultimate act of wellbeing. One day the sleep we enter will be a final breath and the new day will dawn, face to face with Jesus. The more I learn to wake and sleep and let him be God, the more ready I will be for the day when waking and sleeping is all I can do.

At one of the fantastic Fresh Streams annual conferences[5] that I attend, I heard Ajith Fernando share from his vast experience of leading Youth for Christ in Sri Lanka. He shared about the amazing work and miracles. But the thing that stuck with me was what he said about prayer and the end of life. He talked about prayer being the best thing we do in our lives so that when it is all we can do, that will be a promotion.[6]

Wow!

I want to learn to practise now for that day. I want to learn how to dwell in Christ; how to make the only thing I will one day be able to do into the best thing I do now.

So that one day when I sleep that last sleep I won't be clinging onto things I didn't need anyway.

A word of caution here when dealing with folk who feel life is too hard to live. All this talk of peaceful death can be very unhelpful. I am not saying here I would prefer death. I want the fact that one day I will let go of all this to affect the way I am awake to it now. That final sleep, when it comes, is in God's timing. I long to see everyone know how very precious their days are, but I have spent a lot of time around those who would rather just sleep and not be awake.

I want to learn how to talk wellbeing around these people too. I want to be as real as I can and as hopeful as I can, but never ever to exclude someone because they can't muster the enthusiasm to live. This wellbeing language of Jesus is gentle, not judgemental.

I want to learn to speak Jesus' wellbeing, not mine. I would dearly love for no more people made in God's image to feel so desperate that they can't go on. My heart aches for those who find themselves wanting an endless sleep to make it all go away. This quest for wellbeing habits that work is for them.

 zz ...

Especially for them. I have had to take many funerals in my time as a minister but the hardest, the saddest, the most painful grief were the two young men whose families had to say good-bye, without knowing why they had not been enough to give any hope to them.

When I say it's 'OK not to be OK' there is a point at which that no longer feels enough. This is that moment. For those without any hope who just want to sleep forever, it matters that I keep on digging into this subject of wellbeing and inviting everyone to speak it, share it, live it. I don't know of a more vital task for the church than this language-learning. I long for honesty and truthfulness and belonging for all, so that re-gardless of how anyone is feeling they can find acceptance and the only sleep they take is the one where they open their eyes feeling more refreshed, more hopeful, or the one at the end of their God-ordained days when they sleep peacefully and wake in his presence. Sleep. Rest. A sign of wellbeing if ever I saw it. Something to practise so I'm ready for the last one.

'Come to me, all you who are weary . . . and I will give you rest', Jesus said (Matt. 11:28). To sleep, rest, means we are trusting someone else to be in control.

Get Active

These rhythms of wellbeing that enable us to sleep peacefully are best practised, I believe, in community. I know it is possible for many to just look after themselves well, to have good hab-its, to stick to them day in, day out. I just haven't met many of these people. Most people struggle with some aspect of their

291

mental and emotional life at some time. The word 'resilient' gets used a lot to describe those who cope well under pressure and as something we all need to learn in order to have wellbeing.

Actually, it's a word I dislike, though I want to learn from those who write and teach well about resilience. I want to embrace it as a word, but I struggle because when I was unwell I saw it as yet another thing I wasn't good at, had failed at. It has all the weight, for me, of something it would be better if we all were. Something God prefers, even.

I am not very resilient. I am trying to learn habits that help me have wellbeing, be more able to trust God, be more honest. I want to stand with those who never feel resilient, who aren't coping, who just want to crawl into bed at the first sign of trouble. I at least want those who love the word 'resilient' to listen to those of us who don't and vice versa, so that we can make sure we have room for everyone and don't alienate anyone. I think we were made to help each other, to 'one another' each other. Community based on wellbeing levels us all. We are equal. We all have something to bring and share.

> Community based on wellbeing levels us all. We are equal. We all have something to bring and share.

Because we need each other and because I believe the local church has a key place at the table of wellbeing, I am keen that we don't try to make a set of wellbeing rules or try to simplify what is complex. Each person is an expert in their own wellbeing. Each person brings new colour to the picture.

 **Take Notice**

Wellbeing looks different for each of us. For each there will be a different rhythm to this waking and sleeping. For us to find that together, to offer it to our communities, we need to know what wellbeing means for us.

Here are some quotes from hosts and regulars from the Renew family around the UK.

Wellbeing looks like being the best I am that day and not being judged for it.
Margaret

Wellbeing for me looks like sitting with others and knowing that together we get it without judgement.
Anne

Wellbeing for me looks like sharing cake, playing dominoes and laughing with a group of people who care about me.
Ellen

Wellbeing for me looks like a comfy sofa and lively conversation.
John

Wellbeing for me looks like a happy face to embrace the good or bad I face.
Andrew

Joining the Renew family helped me find a safe place to cope with grief and loss when at times it threatened to drown me and suck me into the darkest place.

Liz

Slowing down rather than speeding up when there feels too much to do.

Karen

Renew Wellbeing is a place where I am known and loved just as I am.

Arnie

Wellbeing to me is now to take a pause throughout your day just to stop and breathe.

Debs

Wellbeing for me looks like planting some little plants and watching them grow.

Maggie

Wellbeing for me looks like true connection, being valued just as I am and valuing others just as they are.

Erica

Give

QUESTIONS

What helps or hinders a good night's sleep for you?

What does wellbeing look like for you? What does rest look like?

What daily habits do you have, or would you like to try, to help you attend to your wellbeing day after day?

PRAYER

How is it that although you have surrounded me
Since way before day one
I am so slow to learn
The encircling dance steps
Of the Father, Spirit, Son

How is it that
Despite the song of joy
You've always sung

I often feel alone
Deaf to the sound of home
As a learner of your love
I've only just begun

Resources

There are lots of apps that help you pray the Examen prayer. For example:
https://pray-as-you-go.org/article/examen-prayer.[7]

Conclusion: What's in Your Basket?

An invitation to learn a wellbeing language

So there it is, my list of things that I find help with my wellbeing. Twenty-six practices or truths that I feel able to share in the hope that they might feed someone else's hunger for wellbeing.

If ever there was a time to prioritize wellbeing, it is now. Everyone is talking *about* wellbeing, but are we talking wellbeing? Do we have language to see a wave of wellbeing defeat this tsunami of despair?

> Do we have language to see a wave of wellbeing defeat this tsunami of despair?

In the church, are we taking the language of wellbeing on our lips daily as we share the hope of the gospel with those around us who are struggling? Are we speaking wellbeing to our own souls?

The image of the picnics on a battlefield still gives me such hope that God is only just beginning to restore the broken-hearted,[1] to fight for hearts and minds across the wastelands of those left struggling alone. He is drawing us out to bring and share what we have learned in dark places. This picnic that you have packed up for yourself to get you through the hard days could be blessed, broken and shared in your communities to bring wellbeing to others.

If we tuck in first and 'taste and see' that it is good (Ps. 34:8), we will not be able to help ourselves wanting to share what is good with others. The habits of wellbeing I keep talking about are because they are my habits and they keep me afloat.

So I take hold of this alphabet and use it when I need to attend to my wellbeing. This is what is in my picnic basket. I need to eat it and I am more than happy to share it. I also need what you have in your basket. Wellbeing is rich and varied; this is how I stay in it:

I accept myself and the cup of this day.
I breathe deeply God's *shalom* that is all around me.
I accept his crown of compassion.
I dwell in his love.
I empty myself of all that clutters.
I move in towards the family he has given me.
I take time to reflect on where growth is happening.
I grasp hold of hope again.
I pick up a hobby or interest.
I remind myself of what brings me joy.
I accept and give kindness in small acts.
I let lament flow from me when I am sad.
I meditate daily on his Word.
I see my name held within his name.
I remind myself of the One thing.
I try to stay present in this moment.
I quiet myself and am still.
I allow him to renew me deep down.
I stick to the simple ways.

I think of one thing to be thankful for.

I unite with others, realizing I am already united with God.

I stay within my values.

I wait for the Lord.

I return to the spot marked with an X.

I remember he says 'you' are treasure. He is my treasure.

I sleep . . . zzz . . . and wake and start again.

The wellbeing way. These are words and phrases that I have shared with my church family and it became a space that others could share too. What language will you speak and what space will it become in your community?

I know as church we are meant to be communities of wellbeing, speaking words of peace, living lives of *shalom*, being spaces where anyone can find a welcome and a family and a home. If we get fluent with our own language and learn the language of wellbeing, I believe many, many people will want to belong to the family of God's wholeness. They just can't understand what it is if we don't speak it clearly enough and live it consistently enough.

What about you? What does wellbeing sound like, taste like and look like to you? What are your habits and your words? Will you speak it, share it, live it?

We need each other.

We need his presence.

We are designed for this.

Now is the time for renewed communities of wellbeing.

Get out that picnic basket.

Pack up those sustaining habits and truths.

It's banquet time on the battlefield of despair.

The poem below was written during a hard time when reflection on the battlefield becoming a picnic site was helpful to me. I invite you, as I leave you with this poem, to begin to explore what wellbeing means to you or, if you already know, to begin to share a habit or two with others. What you hold in your hands is of value. In good times and bad you have learned more than you think about wellbeing. There is enough to go around.

> In good times and bad you have learned more than you think about wellbeing.

The battle has already been won.

It's picnic time.

Picnic Time

You parcel up your goodness
In portions wrapped in love
And sitting here alone
I feast on manna from above
You give us each enough
Daily bread each day
You've got us through this famine year
You've fed us so we'd stay
At home
At peace
Your words
Our feast

But Lord, this glorious truth of you
Was not designed for foil wraps alone
And every way we've fed on you this year

Has made us hungrier for family and home!
So holding on to what is left in shaking hands
We take our baskets off the shelf
And pack what we have learned in solitude
About ourselves
Into a picnic ready to take out
'This tiny portion kept back for a rainy day
It's time to share with many more'
I hear you say

But these two fish, these hunks of bread
Are they enough to raise the dead?
I know you've held me, fed me, kept me safe
I've known wellbeing in these days
But will it be enough to share?
Can a single portion fill these trays?

But I begin to pack what's left of simple habits that are here
The locked down crumbs of love that fed my faith
And calmed my fear
And as I pack
There's more
Than I had thought, to my surprise
The basket fills with fruits of
Grace and truth and love before my eyes

So pack your picnic
Grab your rug
It's nearly banquet time
In darkest days of loss
You've learned to find the sweetest wine

The richest feast has not been
In the things you thought.
The picnic you hold in your hands
Simply can't be bought

Now is the time, dear church
To hear through your fear
'It's made to share, this homemade food'
Bring what you hold
And in the place you show your face
You'll see *shalom* renewed

Ruth Rice, February 2021

Appendix 1:
Mental and Emotional Wellbeing and the Church: Some Helpful Resources

Friends from various Christian charities and leadership positions within the church have been chatting about how to resource the local church in the area of mental and emotional health. The list below offers an excerpt from a menu of resources and support for any local church concerned with mental and emotional health in their community and church family.

Christian Charities Offering Information, Training and Resources

- **Kintsugi Hope**
  Kintsugi Hope, a charity set up by Patrick and Diane Regan in 2017, exists to make a positive difference to people's emotional and mental wellbeing. Kintsugi Hope regularly holds or takes part in speaking events, raising awareness on mental health and stigma as well as acting as a driving force to open up conversations on topics many find difficult. Kintsugi Hope also trains people to run Kintsugi Hope

Wellbeing Groups in their community in its commitment to reach out to the broken and lonely.
https://www.kintsugihope.com

- **Mind and Soul Foundation**
  A national charity that seeks:
  To Educate: Sharing the best of Christian theology and scientific advances.
  To Equip: Helping people meet with God and recover from emotional distress.
  To Encourage: Engaging with the local church and mental health services.
  https://www.mindandsoulfoundation.org

- **Renew Wellbeing**
  A national charity training and supporting churches to open simple safe sustainable places where 'it's OK not to be OK'.
  www.renewwellbeing.org.uk
  Read *Slow Down, Show Up and Pray* by Ruth Rice, published by Authentic Media, 2021, which tells the story of Renew Wellbeing and provides practical advice for setting up a Renew Wellbeing centre in your church and locality.

- **Sanctuary**
  The Sanctuary Course from Sanctuary UK
  The Sanctuary Course is a free online resource to grow mental health awareness, offering a space to share experiences and tackle stigma. Combining elements of psychology, theology and lived experience, Sanctuary UK offer a range of resources and training to support a whole-church approach to mental health and wellbeing.
  https://www.sanctuarymentalhealth.org/uk

- **TalkThrough**

  TalkThrough offers a combination of resources that aim to equip youth workers, parents, churches and schools to attend to wellbeing issues. Renew Wellbeing is working with TalkThrough to develop training for renew spaces for children, youth and families – Renew Children, Youth and Families (Renew CYF).

  https://www.talkthrough.org.uk

Church of England Resources

- *Supporting Good Mental Health* by Professor Chris Cook. A PDF booklet, also available as thirteen audio reflections, to support mental health.
  https://www.churchofengland.org/resources/mental-health-resources/supporting-good-mental-health
- BAME Mental Health Tool-Kit, provided by the Church of England's Mission and Public Affairs Department.
  https://www.churchofengland.org/resources/mental-health-resources/uk-minority-ethnic-mental-health-toolkit

Resources for Those in Ministry

- Living Ministry Programme, produced by Thrive (Liz Graveling). An overview of self-sustaining in ministry through the pandemic.
  https://www.churchofengland.org/resources/diocesan-resources/ministry/ministry-development/living-ministry/living-ministry

- A Virtual Wellbeing Programme, provided by St Luke's Clergy Wellbeing; trauma-informed content and reflections on the pandemic.
https://www.stlukesforclergy.org.uk/st-lukes-virtual-wellbeing-programme/
- Mental Health and Wellbeing Resources, created by Sheldon Hub, supporting the wellbeing of those in ministry.
https://www.sheldonhub.org/resources

Additional Resources

- Green Health Project – information on gardening on church-owned land for those experiencing loneliness or mental health issues.
https://conservationfoundation.co.uk/projects/the-green-health-awards/
- Disability and the Church Podcasts by Roy McCloughry, exploring disability and inclusion.
https://podcasts.apple.com/gb/podcast/disability-and-the-church/id1548922844
- *The Bible and Mental Health*, a practical and useful book exploring mental health and biblical theology, edited by Christopher Cook and Isabelle Hamley (see Bibliography).

Secular Agencies and Resources

- **Mental Health Foundation**
  Works to prevent mental health problems by community programmes, research, public engagement and advocacy. The website has a wealth of useful and reliable information.
  https://www.mentalhealth.org.uk/

- **Mind**
  National Charity offering comprehensive information on all aspects of mental health.
  https://mind.org.uk

- **Royal College of Psychiatrists**
  The professional body responsible for training and standards in psychiatry. The mental health information section of their website offers useful resources for patients and carers.
  https://www.rcpsych.ac.uk/mental-health

  In addition, the Spirituality and Psychiatry Special Interest Group of the college has a useful archive of papers, available at: https://www.rcpsych.ac.uk/members/special-interest-groups/spirituality/publications-archive

- **Mental Health First Aid Training**
  Provides workplace-based training to support good mental health.
  https://mhfaengland.org

Getting Help

- **NHS**
  The NHS has a list of mental health charity helplines. It also provides access to local NHS emergency helplines.
  https://www.nhs.uk/mental-health/nhs-voluntary-charity-services/charity-and-voluntary-services/get-help-from-mental-health-helplines/

For Young People

- Comprehensive list of organisations providing help for young people. https://www.talkthrough.org.uk/resources
- Run by Youthscape, the Christian youth charity offering resources and information from a faith-informed perspective. www.beheadstrong.uk
- Organization offering resources and opportunities for young people to share their experiences of mental health. www.youngminds.org.uk

Appendix 2:
Rhythm of Prayer: Renew Centres

In Renew Wellbeing we believe the prayer rhythms are the heartbeat of the space set up to practise wellbeing habits together. These are the suggested prayers that many are using across the country in Renew spaces. The first paragraph describes how to use the prayer rhythms.

There should be a quiet space set aside for prayer, attached to a welcoming space for community connection.

Arrive and leave in quietness. Have a clear sign on the door with times of led prayer. Explain clearly and simply what you are about to do. Invite people to stay in the quiet space as long as they like after. (Always offer blessings/prayer/words of encouragement to any visitors.) Each session lasts fifteen minutes. Anyone can lead. Only the leader has the word sheet and encourages people to respond in the pauses between lines with *short* prayers or words. Suggestions in brackets.

Morning Prayer
from Psalm 103

Bless the Lord, O my soul, and all that is within me, bless his holy name. (Speak out his name, bless him.)

Bless the Lord, O my soul, and forget not all his benefits. (Begin to list the benefits, blessings and gifts he has given today.)

He forgives all your sins. (Let him search your heart for any attitudes etc. that you do not need to carry into the day. Ask for forgiveness.)

He heals all your diseases. He redeems your life from the pit. (Pray for anyone in need of healing, rescuing, redeeming . . . situations close to home and around the world.)

He crowns you with love and compassion. (Sit quietly and receive his love for you today. Be filled with his compassion for others.)

At start or end of session: Psalm of the week and meditation. (See www.renewwellbeing.org.uk for weekly psalm meditation.)

Midday Prayer
Psalm 46:10

Be still and know that I am God . . . encourage stillness, calm breathing/posture etc.

Reading: Read consistently through a Gospel . . . a few verses a session.

Our Father in heaven, honoured be your name. (Speak out praise to him.) *Your kingdom come, your will be done on earth as it is in heaven.* (Pray for him to reign in the earth.) *Give us today our daily bread.* (Tell him what you need.) *And forgive us our sins as we forgive those who sin against us.* (Confess, receive forgiveness, forgive.) *Lead us not into temptation but deliver us from evil.* (Ask for his leading and his deliverance today.) For yours is the kingdom, the power and the glory. For ever and ever.[1]

Evening Prayer

Be thankful for the day that has gone.

In what have you seen the love and compassion of God today? (Speak it out and begin to thank him.)

In what have you not seen his love and compassion? Where there are no answers to be had, cry out to God and give him your reality. Where it is your fault, confess it and receive forgiveness. Where it is someone else's troubles, lay them down at the cross.

What have you learned from the good and the hard parts of this day?

Speak blessing over all those you have encountered today and for each other. Use Bible blessings.

For example:

The LORD bless you and keep you; the LORD make his face shine on you and be gracious to you; the LORD turn his face towards you and give you peace.
(Num. 6:24–26, NIV)

May the God of hope fill you with all joy and peace as you trust in him, so that you may overflow with hope . . .
(Rom. 15:13, NIV)

. . . the peace of God, which transcends all understanding, will guard your hearts and your minds in Christ Jesus.
(Phil. 4:7)

Bibliography

Aked, Jody, Nic Marks, Corrina Cordon, Sam Thompson. *Five Ways to Wellbeing*, New Economics Foundation, 22 October 2008. https://neweconomics.org/2008/10/five-ways-to-wellbeing (accessed 5 August 2021).

Blyth, Louise. *Hope is Coming* (London: Hodder & Stoughton, Yellow Kite Books, 2 December 2021, HB, £14.99)

Bonhoeffer, Dietrich. *Life Together* (London: SCM Press, 1954)

Boyd, Greg. *Present Perfect* (Grand Rapids, MI: Zondervan, 2010)

Brown Taylor, Barbara. *An Altar in the World* (Norwich: Canterbury Press, 2017)

Brown Taylor, Barbara. *Learning to Walk in the Dark* (Norwich: Canterbury Press, 2015)

Brueggemann, Walter. *The Prophetic Imagination* (Minneapolis, MN: Augsburg Fortress, 2001)

Coleman, Kate. *7 Deadly Sins of Women in Leadership* (Grand Rapids, MI: Zondervan, rev. edn, 2021)

Comer, John Mark. *God Has a Name* (Grand Rapids, MI: Zondervan, 2017)

Comer, John Mark. *The Ruthless Elimination of Hurry* (London: Hodder & Stoughton, 2019)

Cook, Christopher. Isabelle Hamley (eds), *The Bible and Mental Health* (London: SCM Press, 2020)

Godwin, Roy and Dave Roberts. *The Grace Outpouring* (Eastbourne: David C. Cook, anniversary edn, 2012)

Greig, Pete. *How to Pray* (London: Hodder & Stoughton, 2019)

Bibliography

Jamison, Father Christopher. *Finding Sanctuary* (London: W&N, 2010)

Johnstone, Matthew and Ainsley. *Living with a Black Dog* (London: Little, Brown, 2008)

Kelly, Gerard. *Spoken Worship* (Grand Rapids, MI: Zondervan, 2007)

Lambert, Shaun. *A Book of Sparks* (Rickmansworth: Instant Apostle, 2014)

Lawrence, Brother and Frank Laubach. *Practising His Presence.* (Jacksonville, FL: SeedSowers, 1973)

Linn, Derek, Sheila Linn, Matthew Linn. *Sleeping with Bread* (Mahwah, NJ: Paulist Press, 1995)

Mackesy, Charlie. *The Boy, the Mole, the Fox and the Horse* (London: Ebury Press, 2019)

Main, John. *Fully Alive: An Introduction to Christian Meditation*, ed. Laurence Freeman (Kindle Edn, New York: Orbis, 2014)

Nouwen, Henri. *Reaching Out* (Grand Rapids, MI: Zondervan, special edn, 1998)

Nouwen, Henri. *The Selfless Way of Christ* (London: Darton, Longman & Todd, 2007)

Regan, Patrick. *Honesty Over Silence* (Surrey: CWR, 2018)

Rice, Ruth. *Slow Down, Show Up and Pray* (Milton Keynes: Authentic, 2021).

Rohr, Richard. *Breathing Under Water* (Cincinnati, OH: St Anthony Messenger Press, 2011)

Rohr, Richard. *Just This* (London, UK: SPCK, 2018)

Rupp, Joyce. *The Cup of Our Life* (Notre Dame, IN: Ave Maria Press, 1997)

Scazzero, Peter. *Emotionally Healthy Spirituality* (Nashville, TN: Thomas Nelson, 2006)

Segall, Ken. *Think Simple* (London: Portfolio Penguin, 2016)

Seligman, Martin. *Authentic Happiness* (London: Nicholas Brealey Publishing, 2003)

Swinton, John. *Spirituality and Mental Health Care* (London: Jessica Kingsley Publishers, 2001)

The Northumbria Community, *Celtic Daily Prayer* (London: William Collins, 2015)

Van der Hart, Will and Rob Waller. *The Power of Belonging* (Eastbourne: David C. Cook, 2019)

Wenham, Gordon. *The Psalter Reclaimed* (Wheaton, IL: Crossway, 2013)

Willard, Dallas. *Renovation of the Heart* (Nottingham: IVP, 2002)

Notes

Introduction

[1] Origin of this phrase not confirmed, but thought to be first used commercially in 2011 by Hope for the Day, www.hftd.org (accessed 29 May 2020).

[2] Ruth Rice, *Slow Down, Show Up and Pray* (Milton Keynes: Authentic, 2021).

[3] Abraham Joseph Heschel, *The Sabbath* (New York: Farrar, Straus & Giroux Inc., 2005).

[4] What Works Centre for Wellbeing, 'What is Wellbeing?' https://whatworkswellbeing.org/about-wellbeing/what-is-wellbeing/ (accessed 1 April 2021).

[5] www.renewwellbeing.org.uk.

[6] Rice, *Slow Down, Show Up and Pray*, p. 139.

[7] Five Ways to Wellbeing. New Economics Foundation and the government's Foresight project, http://neweconomics.org/2008/10/five-ways-to-wellbeing-the-evidence/ (accessed 8 July 2021). Permission given to use Five Ways to Wellbeing with thanks to New Economics Foundation and the government's Foresight project 15 July 2021.

A is for Acceptance

[1] Joyce Rupp, *The Cup of Our Life* (Notre Dame, IN: Ave Maria Press, 1997).
[2] Rice, *Slow Down, Show Up and Pray.*
[3] Dietrich Bonhoeffer, *Life Together* (London: SCM Press, 1954).

B is for Breath

[1] John 3:8.
[2] NIV.
[3] John 8:32.

C is for Compassion

[1] NIV.
[2] Psalm 103:4.
[3] https://www.pathwaystogod.org/resources/questions-answers/what-spiritual-direction (accessed 1 July 2021).
[4] https://beingbenedictine.com/2017/06/27/many-ways-to-prayer-walking-a-labyrinth/ (accessed 5 July 2021).

D is for Dwell

[1] Ephesians 5:32, NIV.
[2] Ephesians 2:22.
[3] See also, for example, Isaiah 6:1; Revelation 5:13; Revelation 4:9
[4] www.renewwellbeing.org.uk/getinvolved.

E is for Empty

[1] www.renew37.co.uk (accessed 10 July 2021).
[2] Luke 8:43–48.

F is for Family

[1] Matthew 3:13–17.
[2] Rublev, *Trinity*. https://catholic-link.org/andrei-rublevs-icon-of-the-holy-trinity-explained/ (accessed 5 July 2021).
[3] Genesis 2:18, NIV.
[4] https://www.newlifebaptist.co.uk/ (accessed 10 July 2021).
[5] https://www.mindandsoulfoundation.org/ (accessed 1 July 2021).

G is for Growth

[1] Social Prescribing describes the way that people are encouraged to engage in community activities and the way health professionals help people to take a more holistic look at their care needs. https://www.england.nhs.uk/personalisedcare/social-prescribing/ (accessed 13 July 2021).

H is for Hope

[1] https://www.local.gov.uk/sites/default/files/documents/working-faith-groups-prom-6ff.pdf (accessed 10 July 2021).
[2] Louise Blyth, *Hope is Coming* (London: Hodder & Stoughton, Yellow Kite Books, 2021).
[3] Mark 4:35–41.
[4] From Psalm 103:1.

L is for Lament

[1] Psalm 58:6.

[2] Brother Lawrence, *The Practice of the Presence of God* (New Kensington, PA: Whitaker House, 1982).

[3] See Romans 2:11.

[4] Psalm 116:15, NLT.

[5] See Matthew 5:4; Psalm 116:15; Psalm 56:8.

[6] Christopher Cook, Isabelle Hamley (eds), *The Bible and Mental Health* (London: SCM Press, 2020).

M is for Meditation

[1] https://unanswered.prayercourse.org/about/ (accessed 21 July 2021).

[2] Pete Greig, *God on Mute* (Eastbourne: David C. Cook, 2020, revised edn).

[3] NIV.

N is for Names

[1] Numbers 1:5–15.

[2] Isaiah 43:1.

[3] See Exodus 3:14.

[4] Exodus 3:14.

[5] See for example, Isaiah 9:6; Matthew 1:23; Colossians 1:16; Hebrews 1:3, NIV.

[6] Psalm 103:1.

[7] Ruth Rice, *Slow Down, Show Up and Pray*, p. 156.

O is for One

[1] Open Doors is a charity serving persecuted Christians. They provide support, resources and training. See https://www.opendoorsuk.org (accessed 6 July 2021).

[2] Kate Coleman, *7 Deadly Sins of Women in Leadership* (Grand Rapids, MI: Zondervan, rev. edn, 2021).

[3] https://www.cinnamonnetwork.co.uk (accessed 10 July 2021). Permission given by Mark Kitson and the Cinnamon Team 12 July 2021.

[4] http://www.ellilta.org (accessed 21 July 2021).

P is for Present

[1] Brother Lawrence and Frank Laubach, *Practising His Presence.* (Jacksonville, FL: SeedSowers, 1973).

[2] Ibid. p. 10.

Q is for Quiet

[1] Greig, *God on Mute.*

[2] *The Monastery*, BBC (2005), https://www.bbc.co.uk/programmes/p00cklrq (accessed 10 July 2021).

[3] Grace is a word that describes God's kindness and love towards us even when we don't deserve it.

[4] Father Christopher Jamison, *Finding Sanctuary* (London: W&N, 2010).

R is for Renew

[1] 2 Corinthians 5:1–4.
[2] https://neweconomics.org/2008/10/five-ways-to-wellbeing (accessed 3 August 2021)
[3] https://www.nhs.uk/mental-health/self-help/guides-tools-and-activities/five-steps-to-mental-wellbeing/ (accessed 30 March 2021).

S is for Simple

[1] https://ffald-y-brenin.org/product/rhythm-of-daily-prayer-free-download/ (accessed 30 March 2021).
[2] Proverbs 14:15.
[3] Ken Segall, *Think Simple* (London: Portfolio Penguin, 2016), p. 1.
[4] https://www.enneagraminstitute.com/type-descriptions (accessed 30 March 2021).
[5] https://www.northumbriacommunity.org/who-we-are/our-rule-of-life/what-is-a-rule-of-life/ (accessed 30 March 2021).
[6] www.renewwellbeing.org.uk.

T is for Thanks

[1] Matthew 6:11.
[2] The Daily Examen is a reflective prayer for the end of the day, dating from the early Christian church.
[3] From 'The Temple', poem by George Herbert (1593–1633) https://www.ccel.org/h/herbert/temple/Gratefulnesse.html (accessed 30 March 2021). Permission given to use CCEL website 9th July 2021.

U is for Unite

1 John 17:22,23, NIV.
2 See for example Ephesians 5:23, where Paul in his teaching on marriage says the husband and wife relationship is like Christ with his church.
3 Romans 8:31–39.
4 John 17:21.

V is for Values

1 https://neweconomics.org/2008/10/five-ways-to-wellbeing (accessed 31 March 2021).
2 See James 2:17.
3 For an article written in 2010 in *The Guardian* about car tyres made into shoes, check out: https://www.theguardian.com/world/2010/jan/03/ethiopia-internet-shoe-firm-solerebels (accessed 5 July 2021).
4 You can help yourself to the artwork for this on Renew Wellbeing's resources page. Or check out https://www.broadwaybaptist.org.uk/renew-wellbeing for more about Renew Well in IOM (accessed 10 July 2021).
5 https://www.sanctuarymentalhealth.org/ (accessed 1 May 2021).

W is for Wait

1 Psalm 27:14.

X Marks the Spot

[1]   Genesis 1:1.
[2]   Dave Robinson, Oscar Zarate, *Introducing Kierkegaard: A Graphic Guide* (London: Icon Books Ltd., 2013).
[3]   https://ffald-y-brenin.org (accessed 16 July 2021).
[4]   https://www.northumbriacommunity.org (accessed 16 July 2021).
[5]   https://scargillmovement.org/ and https://www.stjosephsprayer centre.com/ (accessed 21 July 2021).
[6]   Rice, *Slow Down, Show Up and Pray,* pp. 31–35.

Y is for You

[1]   NIV.
[2]   Manx for health and peace.

Zzz . . .

[1]   Psalm 127:2; Psalm 121:3,4; Proverbs 3:24; Psalm 3:5.
[2]   Genesis 28:12.
[3]   Matthew 2:13.
[4]   Acts 10:11–16.
[5]   https://freshstreams.net (accessed 10 July 2021). Fresh Streams is a network of Christian leaders who gather to encourage one another in God's mission.
[6]   Dr Ajith Fernando was national director for Youth for Christ in Sri Lanka. He has written books about this time including *The Call to Joy and Pain* (Wheaton, IL: Crossway Books, 2007) which explores themes relating to this quote that was part of a talk given at the Fresh Streams conference in 2014.
[7]   https://pray-as-you-go.org/article/examen-prayer (accessed 25 May 2021).

Conclusion: What's in Your Basket?

[1] See Psalm 147:3.

Appendix 2

[1] Matthew 6:9–13, author's paraphrase. The wording here for the Lord's Prayer is a mix of various versions simplified for use by all. This has been developed over time in our Renew centres and is proving to be simple, memorable, yet accurate, and is true to the original Greek.

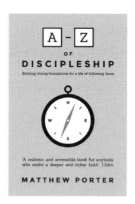

A–Z of Discipleship

*Building strong foundations
for a life of following Jesus*

Matthew Porter

978-1-78078-456-4

A–Z of Prayer

*Building strong foundations for
daily conversations with God*

Matthew Porter

978-1-78893-062-8

A–Z of Discipleship and *A–Z of Prayer* provide accessible introductions to foundational aspects of the Christian faith. Each book provides twenty-six topics to help you grow in your relationship with God.

Each topic has a few pages of introduction and insight, an action section for reflection and application and a prayer to help put the action point into practice. There are also references to allow further study.

Slow Down, Show Up & Pray

*Simple shared habits to
renew wellbeing in our local
communities*

Ruth Rice

How can we renew wellbeing in our own lives and in our local communities?

Looking after our mental health has never been so important. Many of us want to find simple ways to help our wellbeing that we can fit into our everyday life.

After suffering her own mental health crisis, Ruth Rice set up the Renew Wellbeing charity, which helps churches open safe spaces to help all attend to their mental and emotional health. Packed full of personal stories, reflective resources and practical guidance, this book will enable you to maintain your own wellbeing and encourage churches to provide Renew spaces that help local communities journey alongside each other to renew wellbeing.

Be present. Be prayerful. Be in partnership.

978-1-78893-183-0

Authentic

We trust you enjoyed reading this book from Authentic. If you want to be informed of any new titles from this author and other releases you can sign up to the Authentic newsletter by scanning below:

Online:
authenticmedia.co.uk

Follow us: